On Learning to Scull at Forty

BARRY STRAUSS

Rowing Against the Current

A TOUCHSTONE BOOK
PUBLISHED BY SIMON & SCHUSTER
New York London Toronto Sydney Singapore

TOUCHSTONE
Rockefeller Center
1230 Avenue of the Americas
New York, NY 10020

Designed by Brooke Zimmer
Set in Baskerville MT
Manufactured in the United States of America

1 3 5 7 9 10 8 6 4 2

The Library of Congress has cataloged the Scribner edition
as follows:
Strauss, Barry
Rowing against the current: on learning to scull
at forty/Barry Strauss
p.   cm.
Includes bibliographical references (p.   )
1. Rowing. I. Title.
GV791.S88   1999   99–49630
797.1'4—dc20   CIP

ISBN 0-684-84321-8
0-684-86330-8 (Pbk)

Grateful acknowledgment is made to Weatherhill and to the
Cornell University Glee Club for permission to reprint from
previously published material.

Grateful acknowledgment is made to Arnold Guy Fraiman and
the Florida Rowing Center for permission to use an image of a
sculler.

For Michael

Contents

Come, my friends,
"Tis not too late to seek a newer world.
Push off, and sitting well in order smite
The sounding furrows; for my purpose holds
To sail beyond the sunset, and the baths
Of all the western stars, until I die.

—ALFRED LORD TENNYSON, *Ulysses*

Yet my great-grandfather was but a water-man,
looking one way, and rowing another: and I got
most of my estate by the same occupation.

—JOHN BUNYAN, *Pilgrim's Progress*

Foreword

Barry Strauss has done two large groups of people a great favor by writing this thoughtful and affectionate account of his midlife encounter with the sport of rowing. For the rowing community, young or old, rower or sculler, he has provided an accurate and often eloquent description of the rowing experience that we all treasure but are usually at a complete loss for words to describe. For the masters athletes, particularly those who take up the challenge of a new sport in midlife, he offers an insightful account of the excitement, anxieties, frustrations, and joys of discovery and accomplishment that accompany athletic effort in adulthood.

His is a wonderful personal account of his foray into athletics long after youthful vigor, flexibility, and resilience have been squandered or suppressed by the demands of family and/or career.

What rower or sculler can't recall his or her own introduction to the sport? My own came at the beginning of my freshman year at the University of Pennsylvania at the hands of the great sculler and coach, Joe Burk. My very first strokes were taken in the dead water tanks deep in the bowels of the school gymnasium. Even in that unlikely setting, I was immediately intoxicated by the extraordinary sense of power one could obtain while striving to pull an oar through the water, the feeling that I had every major muscle group in my body working to produce force on the oar handle.

That intoxication continues undiminished to this day (although the actual force delivered has diminished rather markedly). It is augmented now by the exhilaration that comes from making a boat move through the water with each stroke. As Santayana put it in *The Lost Pilgrim*, "What is there in the universe more fascinating than running water and the possibility of moving over it? What better image of existence and possible triumph?"

Like many another college oarsman and masters athlete, I too came to rowing with no more than modest success at other sports. My childhood athletic history was one of great enthusiasm, lots of practice, but limited success due to a lack of the skills needed to excel. In rowing, however, I found a sport that demanded some skill, granted, but placed a much higher premium on plain hard work and persistence. College crew coaches still emphasize this point when trying to convince incoming freshmen to take up the sport of rowing. They know that they can teach a willing college student the fundamentals of good rowing and that persistence and determination to master the rowing stroke can more than make up for any loss of receptivity to change that the muscles might have already developed at the age of eighteen.

But what about the mature adult, the thirty-, forty-, and fifty-year-olds who are inspired to take up rowing or any other new sport?

Barry Strauss gives us a wonderfully detailed account of the joys and travails of the process of learning to row long after the flexibility and resilience of youth have been lost. There are no "naturals" at the age of forty! Every attempt at changing the entrenched patterns of muscular activity or learning new ones is met by a phenomenal resistance by the adult body and frustration, soreness and injury are at first much more commonplace than the few brief moments of pleasure and satisfaction.

But those moments do occur and gradually become more and more frequent with time and practice, allowing the persistent masters athlete to enjoy all the same pleasures and rewards that his or her younger counterparts achieve somewhat more readily. And who is to deny that the masters athlete may have gained more from the endeavor than the younger rower? As many a masters athlete in many different sports has learned, there is a special exhilaration and satisfaction that comes with mastering a new skill in midlife, long after one may have thought it no longer possible.

Here is an eloquent description of almost every aspect of one man's introduction to and total fascination with the challenge of making a boat move through water. Enjoy it and follow his example!

> —Harry Parker
> Head Coach
> Harvard Heavyweight Crew

Introduction

To improve the oarsman you must improve the man.
—*Steve Fairbairn on Rowing*

Around the time I turned forty the unfinished novel manuscript went back in the drawer. I dropped the Buddhist mantra I had been worrying over like a string of beads. What I really wanted besides career and marriage and kids and comfort was, I decided, to learn how to row boats and how to race them: four- and eight-man boats first, then two-man boats, then, finally and preeminently, a single scull. If what followed is a story worth telling, it is a tale not of a champion but of an amateur, whose heart was stirred by boats and whose imagination was lifted by history. The oars gave me power but they also taught me humility.

I began to row on a whim a few years ago. A poster in a storefront caught my fancy; it announced a summer learn-to-row course at a local boat club. I had read a lot about the history of oared ships, and I had heard a little about the sport of rowing. Graduate school friends had spoken with reverence of their undergraduate rowing experience. For years, my favorite sport had been running, but lately a string of injuries had cast doubt on my future on the road. So I decided to give the rowing course a try.

It was not a case of love at first sight. The technical complexities of the stroke confused me. If my conditioning was up to par, my innate sense of grace and my ability to concentrate left a great deal to be desired. Rowing was a tough sport and I was not a natural. After a few lessons, rowing might have gone the way of other such midlife diversions as fly-fishing, wine-tasting, yoga, and the saxophone, one-week wonders all. Yet it has lasted. Why?

Certainly not because I became a star. I am a competent rower, but my enthusiasm far outstrips my talent. I kept on rowing, rather, because I love being on the water and because the oars spoke. Listen: they spun poetry out of equations drawn from fluid mechanics. They summoned the ghosts of other rowers, from nineteenth-century collegians to Nile boatmen. Mostly, though, they asked questions, tough questions about who I am and what I am made of. Could I learn to row? Could I row a race? Could I win one? And if I couldn't win, would all the miles on the water logged in, pursuing a mirage, have brought me somewhere worth going nonetheless? After twenty years in a profession, it was sweet to hear a beginner's questions again, sweet enough to inspire the search for answers which the following pages record. Or perhaps they merely lead to other questions.

I hope this book inspires others to row. Perhaps there is a nugget or two here of practical wisdom for experienced rowers seeking to improve their form. I am not an expert on rowing technique, however, and this is not a how-to book. Several fine handbooks do exist, and they are included in the list of Suggested Readings at the end of this book. As a professional historian, I speak with more authority on oared ships of the past. Rowing has attracted over the years writers, intellectuals, and artists. A small sample of their work will be found herein, in both the text and Suggested Readings: enough to whet the appetite, if not to do them justice, and more than enough to demonstrate my good fortune in having such high standards to emulate.

A word about rowing technique. The descriptions of proper form in this book are based on my own experience, on the advice of coaches, and on my reading in the literature. Not all rowing authorities agree, however. Many points remain debated or idiosyncratic. The style may make the man, but men and women make the styles.

I have tried to keep technical terms to a minimum, but the reader will have to master a few. *Rowing* refers to a sport whose practitioners race in light, narrow boats propelled by oars. The practitioners are known as *rowers, oarsmen,* or *oarswomen;* the boats are known as *shells*. Each rower sits midway between the sides of the boat and, in what is known as *sweep rowing,* each rower works one long oar. In sweep rowing, a racing shell comprising two rowers, each working one oar, is called a *pair;* one with four rowers, each working one oar, is called a *four.* The most familiar racing shell, especially in high school and college competition, is the *eight:* that is, a shell of eight oars, four per side, one for each of the eight rowers; there is also a *coxswain,* who steers the boat. Seen from above, the pattern of oars in a sweep boat normally zigzags from *bow* (front) to *stern* (rear), alternating on the *starboard* (right) and *port* (left) sides of the boat, distributing power almost symmetrically. The eight is the largest shell raced today, though theoretically a rowing boat might contain far more than eight rowers. The warships of classical Greece, for instance, were rowed by one hundred seventy oarsmen, eighty five per side, arranged on three vertical decks.

Now things begin to get interesting. Give a rower a pair of two short oars, rather than one long one, and it becomes possible for one person to row a shell by himself. What is lost in camaraderie is gained in symmetry and speed. All other things being equal, a person rowing a pair of short oars will be more efficient than two persons each rowing a long oar. Such a short oar is called a *scull;* two such oars are called a pair of *sculls.* A shell worked by sculls is called a *sculling boat* or a *scull;* the rower working it, a *sculler;* he rows or *sculls* the boat. A shell worked by one sculler is called a *single* or a *single scull;* one worked by two scullers (for a total of four oars) is called a *double* or *double scull;* one worked by four scullers (a total of eight oars) is called a *quad;* one also finds a scull worked by eight scullers (a total of sixteen oars), called an *octuple,* but it is very rare indeed.

Sculling, as such rowing is called, is the main subject of this book. Sweep rowing receives some attention and indeed so do *galleys* (oared ships) of the ancient world, but the heart of what follows concerns sculling. Sculling is not necessarily a solitary sport. But the single sculler, alone on the river at dawn, or spotlighted in his lane during a race, is the most romantic, the most quixotic figure in all rowing. And in a sport in which every rower, whether in a rowing boat or a scull, faces backward—did I forget to mention that?—the Quixote is a hero.

So much for technical terminology. As for personal details, they will occupy more than enough space in what follows. Still, it will be useful for the reader to know now that I live in a college town in the northeast where I teach ancient history at a university. Facing backward, therefore, is second nature to me.

Nobody writes alone. I am extremely grateful to Harry Parker for his generosity in writing the foreword. I owe a great debt to my agents, Glen Hartley and Lynne Chu. I would especially like to thank Caroline Sutton and her colleagues at Scribner for their advice and encouragement.

I owe debts to too many friends and teammates, past and present, at the Cascadilla Boat Club (Ithaca, New York) to thank them all, but among those whom I would like to mention are Michael Bevans, Xavier Buff, Burke Carson, Stefan Cherry, Matthew Clark, Kelly Craft, Linda Godfrey, Herbert Gottfried, Bryan Hoffman, Richard Lungstrum, Bill Reymond, Julie Schuck, Julie Teeter, Mary Elizabeth Vault, and Barry Wintner. I am very grateful to Jan Rogowicz for his coaching and his patience. Michael Flamini, John Hale, Eugenia Kiesling, Ned Lebow, Adrienne Mayor, Josiah Ober, and Donald Webber-Plank read early drafts of the manuscript and provided advice and encouragement. John Ferriss looked over the text with an expert eye. I take responsibility for any errors that in spite of this help may remain. I would also like to thank John Ackerman, Alvin Bernstein, George Bumgardner, Paul Cartledge, Frank DiMeo, Katherine Gottschalk, Victor Hanson, Philip Harris, Mark Hartsuyker, Graham Hodges, Gail Holst-Warhaft, Donald Kagan, Sandra Kisner, Arthur Kover, Terry Laughlin, Ann and David McCann, Tim McKinney, Ronna Mogelon, Lauren Osborne, Mickey Pearlman, Isabel Rachlin, Boris Rankov, Judith Reppy, Nicholas Salvatore, Elaine Scott, Lee Sims, Anne Sullivan, Zellman Warhaft, Margaret Washington, Ford Weiskittel, and the Carnegie Lake Rowing Association.

My parents, Aaron and Diane Strauss, encouraged my writing, endured my athletic ups and downs, and awakened my interest in sports history on a boyhood trip to

Cooperstown, New York. That great lady, my mother-in-law, the late Lila Mogelon, took the time, however ill, to read and cheer my writing, as did my late father-in-law, Alex. My wife, Marcia, patiently endured my absences on the water and carefully read my manuscript. She encouraged me every step of the way. My daughter, Sylvie, and son, Michael, provided love and laughter. While I was writing this book Michael was stricken with a savage illness. His strength and courage in fighting it are the envy of any athlete. I dedicate this book to him.

1

The Practice

Reach for it, and you'll miss;
let it loose, and it'll follow.

—ZEN PROVERB

At six o'clock on a June morning I push off from the dock. Three short strokes with the lefthand oar, a quick turn of the head to check over my shoulder, and the way is clear all along the jetty to the lighthouse. The world and the water are full of promise.

That first moment is always fresh. It eclipses the prosaic reality ahead, five-and-a-half miles of hard work, of sweat and lactic acid and blisters. As you set out, you don't think about how, at a raw hour of the not-quite day, you are sitting alone in a small racing boat—a scull, to be precise—with seemingly no more solidity than one of those balsa-wood airplanes you used to fly as a kid. You could topple the boat simply by letting go of one of the oars you are holding in either hand. You don't think about the absurdity of traveling for an hour seated backward, continually twisting your head over your shoulder for a look ahead on the water, trying not to notice scenery except as a fixed point for navigation. You don't think about the primitiveness of the scull's motive technology: the oars pivot on twin outriggers, a tiny seat mounted on rollers slides from bow to stern, where the feet sit in running shoes affixed to two rectangular pieces of wood dignified with the name of footstretchers. You don't think about the mathematics: how five-and-a-half miles at, on average, an easy pace—that is, a pace of short bursts of speed interspersed with easy paddling and with technique drills—comes to about eight hundred strokes. On each of these eight-hundred-odd strokes what happens is this.

First the sculler creeps into the stern of the boat, then he drives back into the bow. First the sculler coils the body up and then he uncoils it. He propels the boat on the drive by hanging his weight from two five-pound oars, thereby transferring muscle power from body to oar. The legs lead, the back swings toward the bow, and the arms follow. As the blades accelerate toward the stern, the bow drives forward. The boat glides and the sculler relaxes, if that is what you call it, as he compresses his body and readies his oars for the next drive.

It is a movement at once simple and yet as complicated as any ballet, at once natural and yet to be cultivated only through study and sweat. It has its own grammar and language. We speak of "pulling an oar" but rowing (whether sculling or sweep rowing) is as much a matter of pushing. Legs and upper back do most of the work; the arms do not so much pull as let themselves be "reeled in" by the shoulders, as Cunningham says. The body wants to bend at the waist but rowing needs a straight back all the way from shoulders to hips. There is more power to be had by bending at the hips than at the waist, and the straight back protects the lower back from injury. The hip bend doesn't come naturally, though; it takes strong thighs and abdomen and stronger concentration. It takes limber muscles too, especially the hamstrings. At all costs, don't slouch. The sculler should sit up regally at the finish like royalty on a throne.

Everything must be executed with precision in a constant cycle of repetition: recovery and drive, beginning and finish, arms-back-legs-catch-legs-back-arms-release. Every motion aims for grace, for power under control. Blades are to fall and rise from the water with only the merest splashing. They are, moreover, to be alternated expertly between the vertical or "squared" position, in which they catch or clear the water, and the horizontal or "feathered" position, in which they avoid the wind. The hands are to hold the oars gently rather than grip them tightly, even though every instinct screams that anything less than a death grip will send you flying into the water.

The stroke begins with the legs but the back and arms must move along with them. The rower must let the seat slide freely but never independently of the back and shoulders; they must all drive together back into the bow. The difference in the three parts of the drive—legs, back, arms—is one of emphasis more than sequence. Think of a jazz trio, aiming not for three solos in turn but for a single piece in which the accent is now on the piano, now on the bass, now on the drums.

Remember, finally, that this complex set of motions has to be put together into a simple whole. Good rowing has to be smooth and continuous and look easy. Tell a beginner the truth and try not to drive him to distraction: however intricate the stroke, he has to be relaxed. Coaching careers have been made by the ability to get rowers to do just that in spite of themselves.

It all takes place on a boat with the proportions of a pencil, a wood or fiberglass hull some twenty-five feet long and only about a foot wide. It all takes place—to risk stating the obvious—on water. A sculler must not only have the demands of the stroke under her belt, therefore, but she must also know how to maneuver a boat. She has to acquire a feel for the blades of the oar and their behavior, the skills of watermanship.

No, you don't think of any of this at that regenerative moment when you push off from the dock and steer toward the open water. You are happy to have left behind, finally, all the details of launching, from turning off the alarm clock, to remembering to shut the garage door, to carefully lifting the boat off the rack, to securing the oars in the oarlocks, to tying your feet into the shoes on the footstretchers. Mind you, I like the details. They add up to

a ritual, and ritual is comforting and sometimes exhilarat-
ing, like the preparations of a knight arming for battle.
What I like best is carrying a single shell from the
boathouse to the dock while balancing it upside down on
my head. This feat is much less difficult than it sounds.
Racing shells are light, and everyone gets the knack of
carrying them, sooner or later. The sculler lifts the boat
from its rack, where it has been stored upside down, and
rests on his head the footplate in the boat's center, grab-
bing handholds fore and aft of the balancing spot. He carries it thus to the dock, at whose edge he plants his feet
and then gently lowers the boat, right side up, setting it in
the water.

So it is easy to carry a single shell on your head. The
fine points do take practice though. You have to figure out
just what part of the skull to perch the boat on, and just
what spot on the footplate best approximates the boat's
center of gravity. You have to learn how to keep the boat
steady while switching your hands, fore and aft—a necessary maneuver if, for instance, the bow faces south in the
boathouse but the sculler wants to set it into the water to
face north.

Admittedly, a person looks foolish wearing a twenty-
five-foot-long hat, but the feeling of balancing a racing
shell on your head is sublime. It provides wonderful food
for thought, moreover, when having to deal with some
blowhard at work. Just imagine what he would look like
with a boat balanced on his head.

But as you push off, you have forgotten about all work.

You think instead of the Japanese print that the landscape to your stern momentarily becomes before receding rapidly in the boat's wake. You think of the heron that takes off upon your approach, its inky-blue wings spread out like an architect's rendition of the spine of a suspension bridge.

You think of the dawn colors, the red of the rising sun or the gray of the clouds. I like cloudy mornings the best. On an overcast day, with the rain clouds of last night's storm still threatening, the colors of the inlet are muted: the steel blue of the water, the olive green of the willows, the mottled brown of the ducks. If it is dark enough out, the red lights on the long jetty separating the mouth of the inlet from the lake will still be flashing on and off, as they do at night. Often on such a morning, the water is still as a grave. Even the birds, invisible in the gloom, seem silent. Some mornings you are alone; other mornings you are part of a flotilla. Lined abreast and following you, riggers extending out and down from the shell like jointed legs from an insect's trunk, the sculls look like giant water bugs skimming the surface.

A few more strokes bring my boat out of the inlet and into the lake. The daydream stops. I begin warmup drills to loosen the limbs, to practice technique, and to punctuate the individual parts of the stroke. The process of sculling is complex and exact. The single sculler is constantly engaged in a dialogue with himself; he is both pilot and copilot. Is the drive quick and powerful, accelerating from catch to finish? Check. Is the recovery slow, lasting nearly twice as long as the drive, which allows the shell to glide and the sculler to recuperate? Check. Is the body erect but not rigid? Are the blades neither too high nor too low in the water? Check and check again. Nor is the checklist complete if the sculler merely goes over (and over and over and over) the things under his control within the shell. As I row northward, for example, all the while I cast a watchful eye on the boat's trajectory.

The boathouse out of which I row is favored in its scenery but, from the rower's point of view, not its situation. The Cascadilla Boat Club sits in a hundred-year-old boathouse in a park at the mouth of Fall Creek, which flows into the southern end of Cayuga Lake, one of the Finger Lakes of upstate New York. Gentle, deep, and bordered by green lawns, the English-looking creek would be the perfect place to row, but it is navigable only for a few hundred yards upstream. Unless they want to practice turns, therefore, the club members must row out of Fall Creek into the lake to the north. Yet windy Cayuga Lake is no place for a racing single, especially not when motorboat traffic is heavy. Much preferable is the sheltered Cayuga Inlet, another channel just across a spit of land to the west of Fall Creek. About an eighth of a mile wide at its mouth where it flows into the lake, the inlet stretches southward, providing a two-and-a-half-mile-long rowing course. In its southernmost navigable part, the channel narrows to a width of about seventy-five yards. Sights along the shoreline are varied: parks, a bird sanctuary, a golf course, boat docks, several channels leading into marinas, a Coast Guard Auxiliary station, small industrial establishments, a path for bikers and joggers, many trees. College crews have their boathouses and conduct races on the inlet, and distances have been conveniently marked on much of the course.

To get to Cayuga Inlet from the Cascadilla Boat Club you row north into the lake, following the line of a concrete jetty for about three hundred yards until it ends at a lighthouse, at which you make two sharp turns—first west, then south—into the inlet. I know that lighthouse, and I respect it. I know that you have to give it a wide berth as you turn, in order to avoid the eddying currents around it. I know that on windy days it can feel as if you are threading a needle between the lighthouse and the breakwater northwest of it, the waves unsteadying your hand.

Now and then I have found myself in trouble trying to get 'round the lighthouse. Once, for example, I went out in a double scull, foolhardy on a day when my partner and I should have turned back. As we left Fall Creek, the north wind was blowing down the lake at about five miles an hour; the waves were beginning to roll as we turned the lighthouse. It was a beautiful day, though, crisp and blue-skied, and I pooh-poohed my partner's concern about the wind picking up. He was right. On our return trip we could tell right away, two miles up the channel, that we would be facing a powerful wind by the time we got down to the mouth. The wind must have been up to fifteen miles an hour when we reached the lighthouse on our way home. I was nervous at first, and I could feel in his tense strokes that my partner was too. Rowing together truly must encourage thinking together though, because a mile down the channel, I could feel him relaxing at just the time I was. Call it intuition, call it a subtle change in the still-blowing wind, or call it confidence born of a strong performance over a tough mile of rowing. Whatever, we both knew at once, suddenly and firmly, that we would make it. Of course we did end up sweating and tense when faced with rolling waves as we turned the point and with a fierce wind beyond it. For a moment it seemed as if the wind was going to blow us into the jetty, but we rowed out of it. The reward, in the safe harbor of Fall Creek, was smooth water and twenty-five strokes of synchro-nized, confident rowing.

It makes a difference for a man to know that he can negotiate a fragile boat around a headland against fierce winds and churning water.

When my boat is fully turned and pointed southward in the inlet, I generally pause again. I need to check my course, but I linger to enjoy the view. The wide open water of Cayuga Lake stretches northward: a smile on a calm and sunny day, an abyss when the wind blows and the clouds are dark. The lake is a question mark when the fog is just lifting, as often is the case on autumn mornings. As I turn south into the inlet on one such morning, I glide through wisps of mist rising from the water. To the north the mist spouts in geysers stretching above the lake from shore to shore. I am heading southward into the inlet, where the fog is still thick. Here and there a light breeze parts the curtain of haze but it closes as soon as the breeze passes. I turn and see a pair of rowers and when I turn again they are gone, a pair of ghosts. The sun rises and the fog quickly dissipates.

There are traffic rules on the water, the same as on the road: keep to the right, that is, to the starboard side of the boat. I gauge my course by picking a point fifty yards astern of the boat, an imaginary spot on the breakwater across the mouth of the inlet. As I begin rowing southward, I follow the western shoreline of the waterway, turning my head to the bow every fifth stroke to double-check the boat's path, watching for other boats or stray logs. A heavy rain often brings tree limbs into the channel. Boat traffic is usually light at six in the morning, but there are two large marinas as well as two college boathouses on the inlet, and one can take nothing for granted. As the shoreline turns westward, I adjust my stern-side steering point, mentally crossing from breakwater to lighthouse to jetty, then continuing along a line of telephone poles on the eastern shore. My eyes jump from pole to pole, as if running a finger across the tines of a fork.

To turn the boat, you have first to be able to row it in a straight line. Small mistakes can make this more difficult than it might seem. Both blades have to enter the water at the same time, and on the drive both blades have to be pulled through the water at the same depth. Neither foot can exert more pressure on the footstretcher than the other; neither arm can pull harder than the other. The body must stay centered over the keel. Violate these rules and the boat will tend to drift to port or starboard, an error I have spent many a practice correcting.

Once I have rounded the inlet's first bend and reached a place where the channel goes for several hundred yards without turning, I begin picking up the pressure and the pace: that is, I row harder and faster, working by increments to reach full power and speed. After slowing down for another turn, I often build up again until reaching the bridges that cross the inlet. (There was one bridge when I started rowing but new ones have been built since.) If I have pointed the boat well, I hardly have to slow down at all to get the boat between bridge post and shoreline with room to spare for the oars. The bridges resound with the sound of passing traffic. Beyond, all is quiet. The waterway narrows into a tree-lined flood-control channel that extends about 1,700 yards. After passing under the bridges I give my lungs a rest over the next 500 yards by going back to drills, practicing bladework or rehearsing proper body position to keep the boat balanced at each point of the stroke.

Other days I do drills before the bridges and build up the power and cadence afterward. In either case I usually row hard again over the final 500 yards before the navigable part of the inlet ends with finality at the blank wall of a concrete embankment. There the channel veers eastward, flows under a railroad trestle, and over a low dam. I take a rest. I deserve it. I drink from my water bottle. I stretch out on my back, my head toward the bow, holding on to the oars to keep the boat balanced, and I look lazily at the sky. I am invigorated and exhausted in mind as much as body.

The colors of upstate New York are rich but they lack grandeur. The brown is the deep color of mud in a barnyard, the green would content the hungriest cow, the gray is the snow-and-pebble outflow gushing from a plow on a winter highway. The rising sun, however, works miracles. In its light, I catch sight of a blue heron on the shoreline. The bird's uneven gait and mannered stance—neck elongated, beak protruding—call to mind some figure in an Egyptian tomb painting. Dawn paints the Cayuga Inlet in the bright and royal colors of the Nile.

There is a place where cerebral and corporeal meet: they call it rowing. A sculler pays meticulous attention to every bodily motion in order to attain an effortless style. To get rowing that flows you have to know where every motion goes. Rowing is the paradoxical combination of mechanical engineering and the romance of the sea. The rower needs the body of an ironman and of a yogi.

One of the best things about sculling is its mechanical regularity. You can systematically isolate individual elements in the cycle of stroke and recovery and try to improve them, working over and over, day after day. It's a

Roman sport, recalling the regular *thump thump thump* of the legions marching on Italy's paved roads, or the conjugation of a Latin verb: *amo, amas, amat, amamus, amatis, amant.* Yet it's also the quintessential Greek sport: harmonious, competitive, agonizing, nautical, and above all, intelligent. It combines Odysseus's brains and brawn and love of the sea with the tactical precision of a Spartan pikeman.

In odd ways sculling is reminiscent of the martial arts. Not that the differences aren't great. The sculler has to think in order to achieve thoughtless effort. The effect is the opposite of Zen, whose practitioner must be thoughtless in order to think. And yet the two—rowing and Zen meditation share a common dedication, a common escape from the workaday world. Perhaps they share a common language too.

The martial arts masters speak about the slowness with which the body learns, and they are surely right. The intellectual wants to learn to row the way he learns to philosophize, by reading and talking and thinking. The body knows differently. A karate instructor once told me that he was struck by the huge discrepancy between my capacity to think logically and my kinesthetic sense. I took it as an insult, but I took it wrong.

I finally figured that out on the water, in my own stubborn good time. I was trying to conquer my inability to extract my blades from the water smoothly at the finish of the stroke. No matter how hard I tried, I kept feathering the blades before extracting them instead of feathering while extracting them—the proper technique. The error increased water resistance, slowed the boat, and upset my balance and my concentration for the rest of the stroke. I understood the problem. I thought about it, talked it over with the coach, tried to visualize proper technique. Nothing worked.

Salvation came one morning when I arrived at the boathouse and discovered that the club racing boat I usually rowed in was temporarily out of commission. That day I rowed instead in a training boat. That training boat has heavy oars with oddly shaped handles: each fashioned like a bicycle pedal instead of a broom handle. Uncomfortable as they were, the pedal-like handles always let me know the precise location of the blade. When the long side of the pedal was up, the blade was squared; when the short side was up, it was feathered. The key to finishing the stroke was to turn the pedal while pushing the oar down and away instead of turning the pedal first. The experience of *feeling* in the handles what the finish was supposed to be allowed me to repeat the motion with normal oars (i.e., with cylindrical handles). In order to go from intellect to action, I needed to speak to the body in its own language.

Plato long ago knew all about body language. In his ideal republic, the aspirant to wisdom studied gymnastics as well as dialectic. Plato knew that until the body apprehended harmony, the mind could not apprehend the nature of the good. Somehow that lesson had eluded me before I decided to subject a scull to my hyper-intellectual clumsiness. As a student of sculling I am, I suppose, no Westerner trying to come to grips with Eastern pedagogy. I am a lost lamb trying to find its way back to its own flock. I think I am making progress.

It is time to head back down the channel. Drills out of the way, fully warmed up, I am ready for the hardest work of the day. Sometimes I go all out and row at race pace down the entire inlet to its mouth, all two-and-a-half miles, recording the time on a stopwatch. More often, though, the workout is more varied, consisting of intervals of hard rowing (over such and such a distance or for such and such a time, or for ten or twenty or fifty strokes) interspersed with rests. Sometimes I row at a steady but easy pace, which permits constant adjustments of blade handling and body positioning. Now and then another sculler heading in the other direction passes into my line of sight; if her or his form is good, it jogs me into correcting my own.

Any of these workouts is demanding; none leaves room for error or for daydreaming. The sights of the inlet march by in turn. Trees, bridge, coast guard station, boathouses, city park with its playing fields, marinas—my eyes neglect them, one and all. A sudden slapping sound: is it my starboard oar? No, just an inconsequential duck diving for a fish. Steering requires my continual attention. I begin by lining up the stern with a telephone pole at the far end of the inlet. As the channel turns, I constantly pick new points on shore by which to steer. I must nonetheless keep on turning and checking over my shoulder on every fifth stroke. If I get overconfident and wait to the tenth or fifteenth stroke, it might be too late to avert a crash with another boat that has wandered out of its lane. If I lose my concentration, I might stray out of my own lane.

Steering requires continual attention. Fair enough, as one would neither expect nor desire to scull on automatic pilot. Fair enough too that a certain amount of physical discomfort is a continual reality: that one cannot stop in the middle of a piece to wipe the sweat off the forehead or a mosquito off the arm; that one has to row equally well bundled up in a cap and sweatshirt in March or thinking of the water bottle in July; that if the waves are bad enough you get dizzy. But is it fair enough that breathing requires continual attention? That holding one's breath is a constant trap for the beginner, that the sculler must establish a regular rhythm of inhaling and exhaling, a rhythm that he may constantly have to remind himself of as he practices—is that fair?

Sure. No one said it would be easy. That less-than-profound reflection brings me to a question that my wife asks me. So do my parents, my friends, my colleagues, and even perfect strangers. Indeed, I myself sometimes ask: why? Why do I keep at this impractical, expensive, exhausting, time-consuming thing? Why do I drag myself out of bed at 5:30 in the morning when I could be sleeping in? Why do I subject myself to criticism from disapproving coaches—I, the last man on earth to take criticism well?

Because it's beautiful. Because it's challenging. Because it's escapist: when I'm on the water, I'm on the water and nothing else matters, not the kids or the bills or the students or the committees, not everything else that takes away time day after day. Because the secret of leisure is to find work that is play. Because it's egotistical, a navel gaze at physical and psychological flexibility and toughness. Because it's a fantasy, a mythic odyssey aimed at a point somewhere between a Viking harbor and the womb. Because it's elitist, an initiation into arcana. Because it's nostalgic, rowing being a skill not much in demand in the industrial world. Because it's fragile: the boat club is run on a shoestring, and the beat-up old boats held together by spit. Because it's dangerous, and exercises the wits against the wind and the water. Because it's a ritual. Because it's redemption.

For many years, my life was a story about the Little League. Not the usual story of sunny memories, eternal summers, and father-and-son games of catch. No, my Little League consisted of strikeouts and left out, two interminable seasons' worth. Games where I stood in the outfield thinking about how badly I wanted to be somewhere else, focusing on the taste of the cherry colas or lime rickeys which the coach would take us all for afterward, praying that nobody would hit the ball into whichever corner of the outfield they had put me in. I practically closed my eyes during my turns at bat, since I had already given up before getting anywhere near the plate.

But many kids have crummy experiences in the Little League. Why was I so sensitive about mine? Why did the wound sting so? Why did I live in terror for so long that someone would find out the horrendous truth—that I threw "like a girl"? Nor should I use the past tense. Whenever I go to a picnic today where softball is on tap, I usually get a friendly invitation to join the game and usually beg off in a friendly and self-deprecating way: "I have too much respect for the game to inflict myself on it," I say, or some such thing, but my smile is deceptive. I feel like I am strapped to a chair, spotlight glaring, everyone watching, everyone laughing. Even now, in my forties, even as a successful professional, even if I admit affection for baseball—by far my favorite professional sport—I am still a terrified eight-year-old alone on the windswept plain of Mudville.

I do not know the answers to my questions. Two things are certain though. One is that if I hadn't struck out in the Amity Little League I would no doubt be less of a fixture at the Cascadilla Boat Club. The other is that the balm heals.

On the final stretch of the return trip down the inlet, I am back at the jetty again, this time rowing on the eastern side of the channel, opposite the shore I hugged on the trip out, and going in the opposite direction, heading north toward the lighthouse. I am sculling hard, sucking in great breaths on each recovery and forcing them out gustily on each drive. My heart is racing, my legs are burning, my fingers are tightening their hold on the handles. As I grow tired, my upper back and shoulders tend to tighten. My concentration ebbs; I start to rush the slide on the recovery. Slow it back down, I say to myself. Let yourself feel the boat glide between strokes. My body listens; I can immediately feel the difference in the restoration of proper form. I feel more efficient, more confident, and the boat goes faster.

The feel of a good row stays with you for hours afterward. Your muscles glow, your mind wanders from the papers on your desk and goes back, again and again, to that terrific power piece at the end of the workout when it felt as if you and the boat were flying, as if your legs were two cannons and your arms were two oars and the great lateral muscles of your back were pterodactyl wings and the brim of your baseball cap was a harpoon. As if you were a prehistoric animal racing over the water, growling over the big fish you had picked out to claw with the talons of your feet, flapping wings humming at a baritone pitch as you ready to dive and spear your prey. On the water such fantasies are fleeting, because the water constantly demands an alert brain. Give in to mindless brawn even momentarily and you might find yourself missing a stroke and flipping into the water, or heading for a crash with a stray log or another boat or the shore.

Thoughtlessness is for hot tubs, not rivers. The sculler sits relaxed and confident but mindful, as anyone would be who had to look behind his shoulder to see where he was going. He is continually scanning the water ahead and thinking about his next move. Sculling is both an endurance sport and a craft. No wonder that sculling races involve as much strategy as they do muscle power and conditioning.

As the bow of the boat reaches the lighthouse, I take my last hard stroke. Immediately I switch to an easy paddle pressure. I am gulping in air, stretching my back, looking around, enjoying the slight breeze off the lake, but still sculling, easily now, as the boat continues northward. I begin pulling harder on port in order to move the boat first eastward and then southward, away from the breakwater and back toward the other side of the jetty and the mouth of Fall Creek.

Once I have rounded the lighthouse and repointed the boat, I begin sculling again. My strokes here are usually slow and deliberate, accurate and relaxed: as if my body has breathed a sigh of relief to be on the last leg of the trip. I catch the water cleanly, accelerate the drive smoothly, with blades at just the right depth, and release the oars, it seems, with hardly a splash. As often as not I am heading into a light wind, whose mild resistance helps steady the boat, even if it also requires more effort to keep up speed. Although it is still necessary to check over the bow every few strokes, boat traffic is lighter here than in the inlet, so my mind is less resistant to the purely aesthetic

details of the surroundings. Each turn of the shoreline
and of the boat changes my angle of vision slightly, as if
watching a continuous series of freeze-frames. First come
the green hills to the north; they frame Cayuga Lake like a
double row of columns merging at a vanishing point on
the horizon. The boat turns, and beyond the concrete
jetty there appears a thicket of masts in a marina adjoin-
ing the inlet. Another turn reveals a gull perched atop
each of the telephone poles that march down the jetty. A
swing of the boat toward port, to avoid a tumble of over-
hanging branches, and I enter the mouth of Fall Creek.
The insistent twitter of swallows reverberates from tree to
tree.

Sheltered from the wind, the water in the creek is as
smooth and polished as the crown jewels on coronation
day. I row southward past the dock, trying now to make
every stroke count, every stroke as technically good as possible. I am slowing down. A few more strokes and it will be
time to put on the brakes, that is, to hold the oars squared-
up and stationary in the water, thereby bringing the boat
to a halt. I stop just short of a cluster of water lilies. A
quick pivot, an easy row back up toward the boathouse
and, in the end, a gentle glide alongside the dock, which I
reach out to touch with my palm.

I am home.

2

The Beginner

A boat is the hardest thing I know of to put into
perspective. It is so much like a human figure,
there is something alive about it.

—THOMAS EAKINS

Off season on a rainy December day I stand on
land opposite a single scull, its bow coming
directly at me. The boat is beautiful. The dark-
varnished hull is made of African timber, the framework
of spruce, while the riggers are stainless steel. The two
fiberglass oars have been artfully fastened in place in the
oarlocks as if heading for the catch.

We are indoors. The scene is an art gallery, not a
boathouse; the occasion an exhibit of paintings on the
theme of rowing. My presence is purposeful. I have made
a long overland trip by bus, train, and taxi because I
wanted to look at pictures of boats. Most of the other

gallery-goers, however, have wandered in from the neighborhood, innocent of rowing, as their comments indicate. They turn from the paintings and drawings to the single scull, itself a work of art to put pause to the skeptics who might wonder what rowing could offer an artist. The spectators gather around the scull and yield to the elegance of its clean lines, probably for the first time.

"How fast do they go? It's a beautiful shape, isn't it?" a woman says to her companion. He nods, head bowed. Others stop and position and reposition themselves to admire the boat from various angles. Watching them reminds me of my excitement the first time: if not the first time I saw a single scull—to be honest, I don't remember when that was—then the first time I looked at a racing single with the appraising eye of a novice rower, knowing that soon I would have to prove myself in this sleek and precarious vessel.

I had already been rowing for several months then in four- and eight-person sweep boats. Like most Americans, I learned to row sweep before learning to scull. In European countries the sequence is usually reversed, and novices learn the skills of balance and control in a sculling boat before stepping into a sweep boat. Americans prefer to let beginners learn the ropes first in sweep rowing before advancing to the greater technical challenge of sculling. Besides, most rowers belong to high school or college crews, where the vast majority of competition is in sweep rowing. Masters rowers, however, especially in a small town, find it difficult to arrange a regular time when four or eight people, plus a coxswain, all busy adults, can meet for practice. Many masters rowers, therefore, find a single or double scull more practical than a sweep four or eight. You can row a sculling boat alone but not a sweep. For two rowers, a sweep pair (that is, a sweep-oared boat with two rowers) may be a good alternative to a double scull but only if the rowers are talented or well practiced, because the layout of a pair leaves little room for error. It is easier for one person to work two oars, as in a single scull, than for two people, as in a pair. Anything less than perfect coordination between the two rowers in a pair will slow the boat or bring it off course.

Sculling, therefore, tends to be the choice of masters rowers, for all the reasons stated and for another too. Sculling is slightly more cerebral, slightly less a matter of muscles than sweep rowing. It offers the masters athlete a better chance to test the validity of the cliché about age and cunning beating youth and enthusiasm.

So we masters tend to end up willy-nilly as rugged individualists, heroic tacticians like Odysseus on his raft, aristocrats sitting with regal bearing in our own boats, rather than team players keeping time together. We began, however, like the high school kids, rowing sweeps.

Wars have broken out with less clarity than the start of my career as a rower. I remember the precise day, time, place. It was an overcast midday in June, and I was on my feet running an errand in the warren of boutiques, restaurants, and hangouts that spills downhill southward from campus. I passed a Xeroxed poster in a storefront window announcing: LEARN TO ROW, which set off the sound of a slight *hmm* in my mind. At the signal there opened a dossier of associations about rowing, assembled higgledy-piggledy over the years. I remembered the vague impressions from Central Park, from summer Olympics in front of the TV, and from the folk wisdom of the Ivy League: that rowing was a sport for people who had never been good at sports, that it was a sport of second chances and first aid, that it was all about conditioning and all about grace, that it was for people with big thighs and bigger IQs, that it was for Anglophiles and stevedores, that it was both elitist and democratic. In other words, half the things I could think of about rowing directly contradicted the other half. I might have kept on walking but, being an academic, I have a taste for paradox, so I turned back.

It was the right moment in my athletic career, or lack thereof, to try a new sport. I had been a runner before running had acquired its Zen popularity, but my long association with the sport was nearing its end, thanks to one injury too many. Cycling had never quite grabbed me, and lifting weights bored me. It was time for a change.

And then there were the Greeks. I was in the stretch of my career when it was Greece for breakfast, Hellenism for lunch, Homer for cocktails, and the-folks-who-had-a-word-for-it for dinner. Ever since graduate school, when I had immersed myself in Greek antiquity, I had begun to think like an ancient Hellene. As a result I was perhaps more than usually pugnacious and philosophical, but I was also a spiritual countryman of Odysseus, which meant that whenever a patch of water came into view, the heart began to itch for a voyage, which took a boat, which needed an oar.

My research focused on war in the ancient world. At the time I was preparing to weigh in on a scholarly combat over the speed with which an ancient fleet could have rowed across the Dardanelles. I had read everything there was to read on the subject, in languages ranging from Attic Greek to German. I had thumbed through nautical charts of the Aegean. I had even gone the length, the summer before, of traveling to Turkey and trudging the back roads near Gallipoli, picking up potsherds and looking for the beach on which I might have hauled up one hundred and eighty ships had I been the commander of the Athenian fleet. I had brought my wife along with me or, rather, talked her into coming, because as a trained archaeologist she knew a lot more about those sherds that I did. I had done everything except for this: I hadn't given a thought as to what it might have felt like to row in an ancient warship. Rowing in a modern shell, it seemed, might be the next best thing.

I decided to give Learn to Row a chance. The Greek in me wanted to know what it felt like to pull an oar. The intellectual wondered about how to get eight individuals to move to the same beat. The athlete wanted to check what has been described as the ultimate workout. The

romantic craved seeing if the quirkiness of the sport—
there is after all, little practical value to oarsmanship in the
postindustrial age—stirred his blood. The failed Little
Leaguer couldn't resist a second chance to make the team.
So I copied down the phone number from the poster,
made a call when I got home, and arranged to show up at
the beginning session the following week. The voice at the
other end of the telephone asked politely about my sports
background; rowing, it was pointed out, was a sport that
risked few injuries. So it was, I would discover, but only if
you did it right.

The Learn to Row class had its first meeting at 6:00
P.M. on a summer weekday. There were about a dozen of
us, the usual nineties college town lot: youngish, casual,
noncommittal; countercultural enough to wield chopsticks
at a veggie restaurant but not so bohemian as to stand out
at a Chamber of Commerce meeting. We hung out in
front of the boathouse, waiting for our teacher. She
turned out to be a grad student in mathematics who had
excelled as a college oarswoman—worth waiting for, but if
the boathouse could have talked we wouldn't have needed
a teacher.

I love boathouses. I love them in spite of industrial surroundings. I love them even when they are just Quonset
huts with concrete slabs for floors and walls lined with a
pileup of factory-made fiberglass boats. I love them when
they are prefabs or converted warehouses, whether they
face barge traffic or party boats. Those are mere lover's
blemishes. Not only were they absent from the boathouse

I was to discover that evening, but they were counterbalanced by enough charm to elicit a sonnet from a steeplejack. The Cascadilla Boat Club's boathouse sits in a park where a tree-lined creek flows into a pristine lake. Surrounded by huge, aged willows, its dilapidated, wooden form bespeaks a genteel indifference to appearances, or perhaps a sportsman's intensity of vision: he focuses on the boats, not the building that houses them. Step inside and smell the odor of varnish which, combined with the humidity, suggests a cask-lined wine cellar. Love? The place had me swooning.

The boathouse had been built for a private school long ago, in the 1890s, when New York Governor Teddy Roosevelt, eager to put the imperial back into the Empire State, was exhorting the citizenry to instill manly vigor in its sons. So generations of prep school kids went out to conquer Cayuga Lake. Then came the recessional, a century of Rust Belt winters and the school's eventual decision to sell off its lakefront property to the municipality. The shingles were faded, the gymnasium on the second story rendered unusable, the foundations were cracked, and the back porch sagged. Yet when in the 1970s a group decided to found a community boat club, they discovered that the two boat bays were still intact. Age had left the building not only its primary function but its allure. Look at the half-oval portal of either boat bay, the door slid partway open; look from the water, stare at the dark interior: inviting, mysterious, as suggestive of treasure as the entryway to Aladdin's cave.

If the boathouse was a rhapsody, then the site of our next session was a march. We met at a place called "the tanks." The name suggested a prison or bunker and the decor—tile and concrete, weights and machines, windows too overgrown with ivy to let in much natural light, a smell not of varnish but of disinfectant—added to that impression. Yet the space was the college crew room in a campus gymnasium. No guns or watchtowers, but the place was Spartan in spirit, a warning that rowing is about more than picturesque traditions.

Walk into the crew room and you saw free weights and a variety of machines, ranging from sleek, new rowing ergometers—on which more later—to contraptions out of the twenties. But what dominated the room were two long water-filled trenches down each of which ran a concrete spine with eight seats. These were the actual tanks. The water channel on either side of the row of seats was wide enough for a sweep oar to fit comfortably. A raised wooden walkway ran around the tanks, allowing a coach to observe and comment on the rowers. At the head of the tanks stood a large horizontal mirror, which allowed the rowers to watch themselves at work. At the touch of a button the coach could set in motion a motor to make the water run, thereby simulating the feel of a river. It was useful but raised a racket, meaning that in order to be heard above the din a coach would have to bend down to the level of the rower's ear.

The test of the tanks is utility: they work. Never mind the antiquated feel to the place, never mind that sitting at the catch, waiting for a command to be shouted over the din of the rushing water, you might have been in the turret of a World War II bomber experiencing communications problems with the cockpit. Never mind: following the stroke, looking in the mirror, pulling the oar through water without having to think about balancing a boat, listening to the advice of a coach standing directly at your side, you learned.

At least you learned eventually. A lot of winter Sunday afternoons and predawn sessions in the tanks lay ahead before I would reach a measure of proficiency. A lot of power pieces, rowed all out, were in the offing, as were pyramids—exercises that started easy and rose to a peak of difficulty before dropping down to an easy level again—and other schemes for working the body to exhaustion. How much I enjoyed those. I loved the hot room on an icy winter morning, light from the rising sun just visible through the steamed-up windows. It was in the tanks that I learned how to follow stroke, how to concentrate on the back and shoulders and arms of the person in front of me, how to mimic his proper movements and ignore his bad ones, how to blend my rhythm into that of seven other rowers. At times, when it was hot enough and loud enough and we were rowing long and hard enough, I found my ego slipping away into the group, letting the boat do the thinking and my body follow. At such times I could imagine the powerful ties that bound the rowers on an ancient Greek warship—nearly two hundred on a boat. What tales of teamwork they had to tell over retsina before a fire, ashore on cold winter nights.

I loved the camaraderie of the tanks, but my heart's delight was the thrill of exhaustion. I'm an endurance runner by nature, a flyer. In a fight, I'm a missile thrower: my pragmatic ideal is to land a punch, pull back, and dance. I like to move and move fast. I like motion. I've never entirely gotten over a two-year-old's inability to stand still. For me, happiness is intense activity that burns off all my energy. A workout that turned my back to jelly and left my sweat-stained clothes sticking to the seat and that seemed to have snapped the synapses between my legs and the brain that was trying to tell them, "Time to get up"—that was heaven.

All this lay ahead in the tanks, but I hadn't an inkling the first time. On that occasion I learned little. Rowing is simple if you are an experienced athlete, are in good shape, are loose and flexible, have perfect posture, and have mastered the art of listening with exquisite care. Rowing was not simple for me. I nodded whenever the instructor made a point, as if I understood, but I could as easily have assembled the space shuttle as have repeated the moves she was explaining. While we gathered around she sat down in a rowing machine on the boardwalk above the tanks and demonstrated the stroke. She broke it down into its constituents: arms, back, legs on the recovery up the slide, followed by legs, back, arms on the drive back down the slide. The power comes from the legs and back, not the arms, so much so that a rower could actually pull herself off the seat by the force of her leg thrust. To make her point the coach lifted herself from her seat while pulling an oar. Then she stood up and had us sit down and try to do the same, one by one. I saw and I heard but I did not understand.

"You'll get it," she said to me in encouragement, after a few tries on the seat brought me no closer to liftoff. And I did get it, but not for a long time. Not that day, nor the next, nor the rest of the summer did I understand what the stroke is all about. When eventually I got the sequence down I didn't grasp the relative purpose of each constituent: like most beginners I was all arms, all upper body. Understanding the role of the legs in the stroke took a year and execution took several years more. My body was in no hurry to carry out, when the time came, what my mind had finally grasped.

Thus began a long argument between mind and body about moving my center of gravity downward, from arms to legs. The whole power of the stroke starts in the feet and moves upward through the legs to the back; when it finally reaches the arms most of the work by far has already been done. Until the heels and the knuckles and the neck and the other, merest body parts figure that out, then the brain's knowledge isn't good for much. The truth is that, when it comes to rowing, the body is wiser than the soul. First things first though: in the beginning, not even my brain knew what the stroke is supposed to be like. It took a while for me to understand how little I understood.

My first time behind an oar lacked drama. After letting us try our hands at the rowing machine, the instructor seated us in the tanks. She left the motor off and had us run through the stroke in still water. I had been in enough rowboats to know how to handle an oar so my face took on a look of conviction, but in fact the sliding seat was having its way with me.

Introduced in the 1870s, the sliding seat remains a wonderful invention, because it brings so much muscle to bear on the oar. Without it, the rowing stroke would consist only of the arms and back. The slide adds the power of the legs. The technology is simple by any standard, the end result profound. The machinery is nothing more than a small wooden or molded-plastic seat mounted on four wheels that roll on two parallel tracks on either side of the keel, sternward and toward the bow. Yet like a computer chip, the sliding seat is a force multiplier. It is to fixed-seat rowing, moreover, as ballet is to potato-sack racing. As she slides up and down the boat the accomplished rower looks lithe and graceful. Alas, the sliding seat also multiplies the possibility of mistakes.

Once you master it the slide is easy. Smooth, controlled, powerful, you rock back and forth as gently as if in a high-backed chair with a baby drifting off in your arms. Getting to that point of mastery, however, takes long hours and sore bottoms. I have struggled on the slide, fallen behind its rhythm, hustled to catch up to it with no more success or elegance than a lobster clattering after a gazelle.

I think I have finally got the slide down. Yet even now it takes a conscious effort to get the stroke the way I like it. My default mode is still snatching. I usually need ten minutes of warmup, much of it focusing on the leg drive, before breaking the habit of overemphasizing the arms.

The oar looks even simpler than the sliding seat but requires, if anything, even more practice. Coaches speak of a rower who needs "bladework," that is, who has to improve the handling of the oar, but not of a rower who needs "seatwork." The sliding seat is a technique; the oar, whether of fine wood or coarse fiberglass, is an art. The reason is water.

"Water is best," said the ancient Greek poet Pindar. Water is proudest too. It has no intention of letting an oar slice through it the way it would cut through the air. Water is basic; water is one of the four elements. It has its own rules. The rower need not get a degree in the physics of turbulence, but he has to acquire a feel for maneuvering an oar through fluid. It takes as much delicacy as strength. The position of the oar changes with each phase of the stroke: a complex process whose mastery requires many drills.

On the drive, for example, the blade is vertical or "squared" to catch the water; on the recovery it is horizontal or "feathered" to reduce resistance. On every stroke the rower has to drop the oar gently—or, better, let it fall—into the water at the catch, to keep it just barely breaking the surface on the drive, resisting the temptation to drop it in deep, which only makes pulling harder. She has to extract the oar neatly at the finish while feathering the blade for the recovery, and then to square it again on the approach to the catch, making sure to do so early in order to have the blade in position for the drive. Novices tend to grip the handle, holding on for dear life; it takes time to learn to relax and cradle the handle in the upper knuckles. The transition from squared to feathered blade can be tricky, a matter both of timing and technique. The sweep rower has to learn to feather the oar with one hand while guiding it with the other. The sculler must master the complex maneuver of feathering the blade by pivoting the thumb, which manipulates the oar on the end of the handle. The blade is extracted from the water at the release by dropping the elbow cleanly rather than by bending the wrist; the latter a sure recipe for tendinitis. Not even proper form can prevent blisters, although— unkindest cut—the pattern of blisters lets the coach criticize technique. Blisters on the palm mean a death grip on the oar, while blisters on the fingers suggest an easy hold. In any case, both sets become calluses equally and eventually, often not before fruitless experiments with Band-Aids, which are no match for friction and water.

Only a little of this could be taught in the tanks and even less was absorbed. It requires practice on the water. Fortunately, the great day arrived after only two sessions indoors; well, the relatively great day. However pretty the Finger Lakes, my maiden voyage in an eight-oared shell was no journey into the sublime. The novice is not a tourist; he is much too busy mastering details to notice his surroundings. He has to learn to obey the coxswain, to absorb new terminology, to follow the sequence of commands by which a team of eight people lifts a long and heavy boat up and out of a rack in the boathouse and carries it down to the dock, to learn the more delicate maneuver for lowering the boat into the water, to get his oar into the oarlock—a fine procedure if his oarlock is on the waterside rather than the dockside of the boat. Then to master stepping onto the footplate rather than the hull of the fragile shell and quickly to lower himself into the seat, to count down when ready, to lean away from the dock and help push off, to take a few strokes or, while others row, to "way enough"—that is, rest the oar, blade feathered, on the water. He must also learn to adjust his foot-stretcher and "tie in"—that is, tie the laces of the sneakers attached to the stretcher: all on command, all in unison with the other rowers.

An experienced crew carries out all those maneuvers quickly, crisply, even elegantly. Watch, for example, the crew of an elite eight step seamlessly from the dock into the shell and sit down and push off, all in one motion, all together. It takes the breath away. Novices, by contrast, are more likely to afford belly laughs. Our Learn to Row class certainly did the first time out. We bumped into one another, sometimes with an oar handle to the back; we wobbled and weaved; we backed when we should have rowed; we feathered when we should have squared; we shoveled the water when we should have been just breaking its surface; we daydreamed when we should have been hanging on the coxswain's every command. So us novices: the first time, the second, and many more.

We made mistakes with colorful names: "shooting the slide," "opening up early," "snatching," "knifing," "skying," "washing out," "catching crabs." To shoot the slide means to let your legs drive the seat into the bow while your upper body is still in the stern; the body therefore drives at an oblique angle rather than upright; the muscles of the back fail to be engaged, and the result is a loss of power. To open up early means to pull with your back before you push with your legs; snatching is to pull with arms before you push with your legs. Knifed blades go too deep while skyed blades are too high. Washing out is to let the blade out of the water during the drive before the stroke is finished. You catch a crab when the blade gets stuck in the water. Occasionally, when rowing hard enough, a rower who catches a crab can actually be pulled by the oar handle out of the seat and into the water. My biggest, most fundamental mistake, the equivalent of a crack in the foundation of a building, concerned my posture.

The rower has to sit upright in the seat, as forthright as a plumber's square, as perpendicular as a redwood pine and as supple. The seat contains two hollows or holes into which the tailbone fits, like a ball in a socket, allowing the rower to pivot back and forth easily from recovery to drive. If all goes well, that is: this rower was less a pine at first than an olive tree, gnarled and lopsided. I didn't sit upright; I slouched. I didn't imitate a straightedge; I sagged. Worse, I did so unawares. Oh, I always knew that I was not about to go to the head of the class in posture, but years of looking downward as I walked had left me unaware that the sidewalk was not the sky. That's what comes of too much thinking.

It took years to change my posture. It took injuries. It took mirrors. It took yoga. It took physical therapy. In the end, the only thing that worked was to scare myself into sitting and standing up straight. My best friend was diagnosed with cancer and all at once the restoration of my lower back to health seemed critical. I became an overnight expert on stretching. I found a new physical therapist with magic hands and, all but hammered into place by a now adamantine will, my back became as upright as a Doric column and as graceful as a Grecian urn. It would have done a marine proud—or a dancer. Now, at last, I positioned myself onto the seat the way a card slides into a slot, but that's not the way I started out.

Yet however embarrassing a video of that halting, novice summer of rowing would prove today, the fact is, we did progress. We learned to turn. We practiced drills to balance the boat and to pull together, following stroke. Our second week we broke out from the sheltered creek beside the boathouse: the coxswain let us round the point into the Cayuga Inlet, with its two miles of good rowing, if at times heavy boat traffic. A coach's launch followed alongside, to teach and offer life jackets in case of mishap. Our lurches became less steep, our creaks and moans gave way, little by little, to regular plops and steady breathing.

Not that we were becoming adepts or advocates. I, for one, was struggling. If asked then, "Do you like rowing?" I am not sure how I would have answered. In retrospect I know that the sport had got under my skin but back then, grit, not love, made me go on. I wanted to show that I could do it. When, after four weeks, the Learn to Row course ended, I paid up without hesitation and joined a group of beginners who met to continue rowing two or three times a week.

We had fun, the rest of that summer and fall, even if we didn't register shock waves at the Olympic training camp. We worked our way into racing starts and power pieces, in which we rowed all out over increasing distances. We got to go out into single sculls—unsinkable and hard to maneuver training boats or "tubs" at first, tethered to the dock, then slightly more challenging vessels. I enjoyed all this but considered rowing to be no more than a dalliance. Yet imperceptibly I was falling in love.

That epiphany only came late. Not for a year after I had begun to row did the sting of cupid's arrow become too sharp to deny. It was early spring and my first race. I was rowing in a coxed four at a regatta for college clubs, that is, nonvarsity teams, whose members could be graduate students or codgers like me as well as undergraduates. We loaded the boats on the trailer the night before the race. The next morning I set off before dawn for the three-hour drive to the race site in Ontario.

I left home at six when it was still pitch dark out. As I drove north along the hills west of Cayuga Lake, the sun began to rise slowly out the passenger's side window. Every now and then, as the road curved, light from the east would flash into view, revealing a cross-section of blue water backed by steep green hill, sometimes with a finger of white-gray mist suspended above in the luminous sky. Nearer by, the sun had climbed high enough in the horizon for its rays to crest the trees and to begin to light the fields. It made a pretty effect, particularly when the glow reached a stretch of brown stubble left over from the fall harvest, and the daylight turned the tract into gold. The purity of the colors called to mind a place as far removed from upstate New York as youth is from middle age: it reminded me of Greece. I had spent two years as a student there in my twenties, two privileged periods of adventure and emancipation. A boat race might have been a poor substitute for that youthful flight of Icarus; a North American river was hardly the Aegean. Never mind, the prospect was enough to bring back the taste of ouzo and the sound of Anatolian syncopation and the look of women with olive cheekbones.

Ours was one of the last races, so we launched in late morning. By the time we rowed up to the starting line the sun had taken on its midday intensity. The light was silver, shimmering like summer heat on asphalt or like mercury in a thermometer. We had practiced racing starts, had drilled the officials' commands into our heads, but I had butterflies in my stomach nonetheless. To deflect my nerves I had to let my mind wander, and the words *Ready? Row!* made only a distant thunderclap in my ears.

Once we were off though, I was on. Seated in the bow, I followed my teammates' strokes, pulling with all I had from the start, maintaining proper form through about half the 2,000 meters. By the end I was huffing and puffing because I failed to breathe at every catch. Out of synch with my teammates, I followed my own rhythm. My strokes devolved into an absolute beginner's mistake, favoring the upper body pull instead of the push with the legs. I was exhausted. I suspected that I had a lot to do with the result, which was to come in second instead of winning.

Yet I was well satisfied. During the brief course of that race I had learned many things about rowing and about myself. I had learned about the heart of rowing. The rower needs to know technique and has to be in shape. He won't go wrong by using strategy. Yet what it takes to win races is the ability to reach inside and pull out something to keep you going—no, to go faster—when you have nothing left to give. There's a word for what that takes and the word is not magic; the word is *guts*.

The race convinced me of what I had for some time suspected. For me, the ideal life is one that combines body and spirit, one that joins the intensely physical and the intensely intellectual. I would wither away without the exercise of the flesh.

When you are rowing well and hard, the rhythm of the stroke takes over: it drives your days and restores your nights. It imparts cadence and direction. You feel like you and the boat are one, you feel that no obstacle will put up any more resistance than the water does to your oars, you feel that hard work and grit and mental toughness will always win it for you in the end. You feel, above all, part of a larger enterprise. The loneliest single sculler no less than the sweep rower in an eight belongs to the fellowship of the river.

Let me state differently what made me love rowing. On a visit to the town I grew up in I see a very old friend, call him Ira, from junior high school. We reminisce about another friend, Jamie, dead ten years. Ira recollects what a great talent, what a creative genius Jamie was, a kid who excelled at everything he put his hand to. I get a sinking feeling, taking me back thirty years, to a time when I was always compared to Jamie the virtuoso, and not favorably. Jamie the pianist, Jamie the artist, Jamie the writer. Well, damn it, admittedly, my work has always had a clunky side. I've always liked to keep the training wheels on: to ground my writing in research. I've always painted by the numbers. I've never felt comfortable flying free. I'm not Icarus. But there's no shame about it if a man has to struggle. Maybe some can clap their hands and make the rain fall and the crops grow. Maybe so, yet a man is no less a man if he has to get up before dawn, day after day, and hitch the horse to the plow and follow a trail of shit and flies, in fair weather or foul, in order to have food to put on the table.

I come from a long line of men who were neither heroes nor prodigies but who put in an honest day's effort. I come from a house of diligent workers, of right-hand men, of steadfast soldiers: infantrymen in the U.S. Army in both world wars, foot soldiers, guys with sore feet. Give us a chance and we'll end up doing not just honest work but noble work. We don't reach for the stars, we don't soar, but we do row. The first time I touched the handle of the oar I might have been shaking hands with an old friend. That's what I love about rowing. It's so regular, so trustworthy. Rowing, like democracy, is about ordinary men called to extraordinary effort.

I become interested in the small European town from which my grandfather emigrated to the United States early in the century. I learn that a historical archive has a collection of old photos from the place, so I make an appointment to see them. There I find that the pictures have been copied onto a videodisc. As I click the mouse, a procession passes by: village idiots, notables, housewives, peddlers, merchants, water-carriers, musicians, beggars, street urchins, teachers, divines, and politicians. Then comes an arresting sight: an excursion in the early summer of 1920, nine young people on the river in a rowboat. One of them looks the very image of my great-aunt, whom I know only from pictures; she died years before I was born. I begin to wonder if rowing might not be in my blood.

If you are going to write about rowing, sooner or later you are going to have to think about your predecessors. The greatest poet who ever wrote about rowing is Virgil, the greatest historian is Thucydides, but the greatest imagination ever to turn its attention to the sport is that of a painter, Thomas Eakins. Not long ago the Yale University Art Gallery put together a show, the first of its kind, of Eakins's rowing paintings. So a rainy December day found me on the New Haven Railroad, looking out at the dreary Connecticut landscape as the train from New York City headed east. I might have preferred to pass the day going from Manhattan coffeehouse to coffeehouse, which is how I like to spend my treasured trips to the city, but this sport demands sacrifice.

Before setting out I had studied the exhibition catalog, *Thomas Eakins—The Rowing Pictures,* edited by Helen A. Cooper, an art historian at Yale who organized the exhibit. Fine scholarly writing details Eakins's mastery of artistic technique, the precision of his draftsmanship, the accuracy of his knowledge of rowing—he was a rower himself. The catalog illustrations show the strength of Eakins's composition, the purity of his lines, the variety of his use of light. But what the catalog depicts is miniatures. I wanted to see the paintings big and close enough to touch. I wanted to see the cracks in the varnish.

The catalog reproductions in fact did little justice to the paintings on display, but how could they? The biggest of the paintings, like *The Biglin Brothers Turning the Stake* or *The Champion Single Sculls,* dominate the room and even the smallest of them, like *The Schreiber Brothers (The Oarsmen),* draw you in. It is trite, but the most striking thing about

Eakins's paintings is just how beautiful they are in real life. The combination of geometrical precision and luminescent color entrances. This is magic.

Although presumably not rowers, the other museum-goers that day also fell under Eakins's spell. They spoke with more animation than is usual in a museum, pointing and shifting position to improve the view of races and practices. They cherished Eakins's technique—"He worked like a dog!" one observer announced to a friend—and marveled at the athletic form of his subjects. They allowed the painter to charm them with works at once life-like and idealized, a mixture of matter-of-fact realism and a romantic arrangement of light, setting, and mood. The experience of viewing Eakins's paintings falls somewhere between watching a regatta and entering a cathedral.

Look, for instance, at what may be Eakins's most striking rowing painting, *John Biglin in a Single Scull,* an oil on canvas of 1874. The work focuses on the sculler, seen from the side, as he heads steadily toward the catch. An athletic champion of the 1870s, Biglin is lean and powerful, with a rower's characteristically prominent upper back muscles. Intent on his work, Biglin cuts a figure as a stern competitor. Neither his thick mustache nor the red bandanna tied around his head, which on another man might look jaunty, detracts from the seriousness of his demeanor.

Helen Cooper writes that Eakins turns Biglin into an icon of American athletics. So he does, and let it be added, an icon in the religious as well as the secular sense of the term. The painting might be a stained-glass window, an idealization of not merely the compleat sculler but the holy sculler. "Pray for us, Saint Sculler": so might one address Biglin. A rowing shell tends to call for horizontal compositions but this painting is, unusually, vertical—twenty-four and three-quarter inches tall by sixteen inches wide. The result emphasizes the sculler's upright posture and it draws the viewer upward. The painting ascends from the brown shades of the water, in which the scull is reflected, to the brown shell, to the white of Biglin's shirt and to the shining blue of the sky. It is the oar and Biglin's flesh itself, exposed in his legs and arms, that serve as the transition points between the two color schemes. Through Biglin, Eakins turns water into wine.

Biglin himself would have made an unlikely miracle worker. Like the other rowers whom Eakins admired, Biglin was no aristocrat. In fact, he worked as a physical laborer; he was in turn a fireman, mechanic, and boatman. All the better for the painter's iconoclasm. Although he had studied in France, Eakins relished the role of American rebel. Unlike European painters of the sporting life in his day, Eakins rejected gentleman athletes as his theme. Instead, he took a subject that had been the stuff of illustrated weeklies and the penny press and turned it into fine art. Eakins celebrates not fire from heaven but honest sweat, not genius but hard work. The catalog notes that for Eakins, the rower embodied the common man as hero. Cooper writes: "Ultimately, he came to see rowers—in their pursuit of excellence, their drive to break old boundaries, and their commitment to hard work—as symbols of a democratic, American morality."

At Eakins's hands, rowing is not just a sport, it is a creed. It is a calling. To the accomplished rower, it stamps on achievement the seal of transcendence. To the beginner, it is an invitation to find meaning in the most mundane act. Look, for instance, at Eakins's portrait of Max Schmitt in *The Champion Single Sculls* of 1871. Schmitt was a rowing champion and a friend of Eakins. The painter shows him at rest in his single during a quiet moment on the river. Schmitt lightly holds the oars, which are feathered and resting on the water, in his left hand. His right hand rests on his thigh. He looks easily over his right shoulder. The oars form a low triangle on the water line, with Schmitt's upright form bisecting the apex. Oars and sculler are reflected in the glassy water. The overall effect is precise yet peaceful; it is an idyll of technique. Relaxed and in control, Schmitt is going somewhere, but he can choose his destination leisurely. He is going with grace. *The Champion Single Sculls* suggests that the greatest prize a rower can win is not a gold medal but self-control.

Eakins painted the way a rower rows. As the catalog points out, he worked hard at his technique, over and over, until he perfected it. The rower will conquer the river, he believed, and so Thomas Eakins would conquer his canvas. Whatever it took to lend verisimilitude to his art—be it sketches in charcoal or studies in oil or the precise grid of an architect in the preparation of the canvas for oil—

then that is what Eakins would do. He was a pragmatist, child of the great age of invention and rolled-up sleeves of the late nineteenth century. It was a great age of rowing too. In port and river cities it was only a generation or so since watermen had rowed commuters from place to place, as they had in New York or Charleston harbors, for example. The quintessentially pragmatic and egalitarian sport that developed from races among professional ferrymen was in its heroic heyday when Eakins painted. Between the end of the Civil War and the rise of major-league baseball, rowing generated crowds and corporate sponsors, prize purses and telegraph bulletins, stars and scandals.

Eakins bids the novice to take part in a sport that is just one step away from work. Looking at his painting of Biglin reminds me, for example, of something that comes to mind when training hard for a race, day after day: using my body to earn a living. Biglin recalls another image, an old book illustration I recently saw, a tinted, nineteenth-century print of two Turkish boatmen rowing an old-fashioned wooden boat. The oarsmen are lean and mustachioed, their faces marked by prominent Central Asian cheekbones. They wear plain clothes and red caps. Swinging together in time in their long, narrow double, they seem to glide across the Bosphorus toward some castle on the far side. I wouldn't mind a job like that. Out in the fresh air all day, a boatman is spared the deformed privileges of a desk job.

Yet as wide a gulf separates the Turks from Biglin as it does Biglin from me. Let us not romanticize the back-breaking grind of the laborer. When I wake up to aching bones and muscles I can vary my training schedule or take the day off. Biglin could put his tools aside from time to time to compete for the victor's purse in a regatta. The Turkish boatmen had to haul cargoes or pashas across the straits day after day, no matter how much their backs hurt or how much the work began to bore them. What training hard offers the intellectual is not the drudgery of the worker, but rather the aristocratic ideal of the ancient Greeks and Romans: a sound mind in a sound body.

I may be approaching the secret of Eakins's genius. For all the mechanical precision of his artistry, Eakins is deeply sentimental. The attention to detail combined with the mathematical accuracy of the perspective and the dynamism of the motion gives the paintings the authenticity of photographs, whereas the dreamlike light, the hazy backgrounds and, perhaps above all, the idealization of the rowers turn the works into a kind of rowers' utopia. Eakins believes in the triumph of man over machine. In the rowing boat he carves out a small space in which the individual can make a difference by his intelligence and elbow grease. He creates the romantic image of the rower as hero, the rower as conduit between man and machine, the go-between who, through brain, muscle, and dedication achieves harmony between nature and industry.

The same poetry can be found in *The Pair-Oared Shell* of 1872; even in Eakins's repertory the painting stands out for its charged motion, brilliant light, and precise composition. The subject is the Biglin Brothers, John and Barney, rowing a pair, that is, a sweep boat with two rowers, each working one oar. The scene is the Schuylkill River in Philadelphia, just before sunset on an early summer evening. The boat is passing under a bridge, beside a massive stone pier. It has just come out of the shadow and back into the light, where the rowers' reflections in the water are artfully placed. The painter captures the rowers in middrive, legs pushing, arms extended in the power part of the stroke. They look like big, strong guys, these Biglins, but they might be dancers, perfectly harmonious and in time. They have achieved swing that makes the boat look like it is levitating, floating on light above the water.

Eakins is a master of perspective. In *The Pair-Oared Shell*, for example, he presents details of such mathematical precision that the scholar can calculate the time as 7:20 P.M. in early June or July. *The Pair-Oared Shell* might have the strongest lines of all the rowing paintings, between the scull and the oars and the upright rowers and the pier. Eakins is also a master depicter of motion. The boat is a serpent, at home in the river. There is music to this painting and tension, between the engineering exactness of the rowers and the romanticism of the near-sunset colors. The dominant hues are silver, gray, and brown.

Days later I still dream about *The Pair-Oared Shell*. It

captures the sport. Here are the coordination, the swing, the drive, the smoothness, the power. Here is an ideal for a beginner to work toward. Eakins's intimacy with the sport is a joy to the rower. Eakins is not just a painter: he is a coach.

3

The Coach

Teaching
beyond teaching;
No leaning
on words and letters.
                                   —*Zen proverb*

I've known coaches who scowl and coaches who smile, coaches who gossip and coaches who keep to themselves. I've known coaches who goad you with gentle words and coaches who get their spurs bloody. One coach repeats the same point until you get it right, another constantly moves from subject to subject, always looking for an opening, like a boxer, until finally he finds something, anything, which the athlete can correct. Some coaches just punch a clock while others make sacrifices for their sport. They give up their lunch hour or their privacy or even their eye socket: like the martial arts instructor who, during a friendly sparring demonstration with another black belt before his students, forgot to duck a kick. He ended up with four hours of reconstructive surgery on his lacrimal bone.

All in all, I've known a lot of coaches over the years since the Little League. Only during my recent career as a born-again jock though, have I found myself wondering just what a coach is. In Little League days my only philosophical question about coaches was how best to avoid them. The Little League dads who coached our team had no time for me, a klutz who was afraid of the ball, so they put me in the outfield and they left me there. I returned the compliment. Eventually my father tried to rescue my baseball career by hiring a phys. ed. major from Brooklyn College to teach me the basics, but it was too late: only ten years old, I was already too stubborn and too hurt and too egocentric to pay attention. I was uncoachable.

I have come a long way from the outfield. Yet like many a man of forty, I know that I could have done some things better. The years have sometimes left me wondering how I might have mastered life's vicissitudes had I learned long ago how to hit a curveball. How much indeed depends upon what goes on in boyhood between athlete and coach. If someone then had been quicker to hold out a hand or if I had been willing to grasp the hand when it was finally offered, would I be not merely a better athlete today? Would I also be a better teacher? A better father? I wonder and I ask, What is a coach?

To find the answer, I go first to the dictionary. A coach is "one who trains others for an athletic contest, esp. a boat-race," says *Oxford*. To begin truly at the beginning, I look at the word *coach*'s origin, although I know that etymology can be a tricky business. Consider the origin of the word *scull*. Already present in Middle English, scull might be derived from a Scandinavian word meaning goblet or from one meaning shallow wicker basket; either word referring to the curved and hollow shape of the blade of the oar. A more likely source might be the Danish *skovl* (pronounced "scull"), meaning "shovel" or "oar." (This makes better poetry than physics, because an oar is in fact less a shovel than a lever.) Some scholars suggest a Middle Dutch source, while others conclude that the precise origin of the word *scull* is obscure.

The origin of the word *coach*, on the other hand, is clearer, if not crystalline. Coach's primary meaning is a four-wheeled, enclosed cart, as in stagecoach. Hungarians claim that the cart was first built in their town of Kocs, near Budapest; most scholars accept that as the source of the name of what was first called a "coach cart," although the Czechs have their own candidate for eponymous town. In any case, irreverent nineteenth-century college students began calling a private tutor for exams a coach or coacher, that is, someone who, like a stagecoach driver, might get you over a rough road. Soon students applied the word to athletic trainers as well and the irreverence, I suspect, quickly dropped out. Maybe a sculling coach is, etymologically speaking, just a stagecoach driver hauling kids who (in a kind of movable tailgate party) toast each other with upraised goblets and a hearty "*Skaal!*", but nonetheless, when the coach frowns, the sculler worries. After all, a stagecoach driver knows when to crack the whip.

Etymology has its limits. A coach spurs an athlete on, but a coach is neither a hauler of privileged youths nor a driver of workhorses. What is a coach?

To begin with, it is necessary to distinguish essential from accidental qualities. For example, although a dull person can be a terrific coach, some coaches are originals. Consider, for example, a coach with whom I have worked for several years.

Picture him as I have seen him on many early mornings. He sits in the stern of a small aluminum launch, bent over a plastic mug of coffee, looking at you intently through wire-rimmed glasses. He wears old jeans, a rowing cap, and—depending on the weather—a T-shirt or flannel shirt. Gray-haired and paunchy, he has wrinkles to match his years. He has been a graduate student and a schoolteacher and a pilot. At heart he is a tinker; for twenty years he has puttered with and mended the boats of the club of which he is manager and chief coach. Everyone in town seems to know him. He looks rumpled and absent-minded, but when it comes to dissecting a sculler's performance, he is a brain surgeon, precise and analytical and life-saving.

Opposite him in the bow of the launch is a huge, unkempt St. Bernard who is no saint. He can whimper sweetly, but he is not above growling at a rower who heads toward Coach's van: a cavernous, rusting thing that seems to be held together by dog hair and spit, but without doubt a useful thing. It tows boat trailers and holds metric wrenches and bicycles and life preservers and food. Rare is the rower in our club who does not end up riding in the van to some race or running an errand to fetch something from it. I was on one such foray—in search, if memory serves, of a long nail to help put together a makeshift boat sling—when the dog finally lost his patience with intruders. I guess he decided to make an example of me. Anyhow, he bit my bum. All the miles on the water under a coach's eyes must have bred stoicism into me, as I didn't make a sound of protest, but I jumped higher in the air than I ever thought I could.

A coach does not have to be an original, any more than he has to be a poet, but my coach is that too. As he assessed my rowing one memorable morning, he was all but a bard in a launch. "Let your shoulders," he said, "feel like an angel's wings at the catch." At the end of a hard row on a day when I had grown tired and my body was looking more like it was dancing the Charleston than a sculler's ballet, at such a moment, I was grateful for the unexpected touch of the muse. Coach was right, I knew, when he said that I wasn't sitting up straight enough at the catch, and he was right when he said that my vertebrae needed to stretch about another two centimeters, and he was right when he said that I must relax my grip on the oar handles. Only the image of an angel in a single scull though, made me sit up and take notice. I could feel my shoulders loosening and stretching as if pulled by invisible hands. And the light breeze rising from the lake looked now as if it were turning the smooth water not into wavelets, but into feathers and thistledown.

His words come back to me hundreds of miles away. In late August, I am visiting my in-laws on their farmstead in Ontario. I am relaxing, but in the puritanical way that becomes second nature to rowers. Instead of enjoying a chaise longue I am exploring the rolling hills on foot, via distance runs and windsprints, doing push-ups and, strangest of all, skipping rope. Another rower once told me that it was a terrific workout when you were off the water and, as I am discovering, she was right.

I stand in the driveway between the woodshed and the horseshoe pitch, rope at the ready, and thinking that what is good enough for Muhammad Ali is good enough for me. As far as the eye can see I am surrounded by fields of allergens or, as I would prefer to think, by a sea of wild-flowers: by goldenrod and black-eyed Susans, by Queen Anne's lace and purple vetch, by milkweed and bulrushes and by a dozen green and red and yellow things whose names I cannot begin to guess. My jump rope is the old-fashioned kind, nine feet of cord and two wooden handles, which I hold as reverently as I might my oars. I start and stop, a beginner in pursuit of two hundred jumps in a row. I take my pulse against a stopwatch. I pace up and down the driveway, kicking gravel as I go. Most of all, as I jump, I think.

I realize that skipping rope is good not only for building up wind, as every stock photo from a boxer's training camp shows, but for rhythm and relaxation and posture as well. If you don't want to trip over the rope you have to keep turning it in long, graceful arcs. To get them you need to breathe regularly and stand tall and keep your shoulders upright but loose. In other words, you need to let your shoulders feel like an angel's wings.

Let us not underrate inspiration, but let us hope that there was calculation too in Coach's poetry. Say he saw in me the kind of man who appreciates a metaphor more than most, and say that he is an adept of the adage about catching more flies with honey than with vinegar. In other words, say he is a psychologist. Few professions offer skills more useful in coaching. For example, if a beginner is flinging himself from bow to stern you could stop him dead by commenting, "You row all bent over, like a clock maker. You're as twisted as a corkscrew." A psychologist, however, might think twice before sounding off so. A tough-minded coach once made just this remark to me. He was no diplomat, but he had been in the Olympics in his day, and he knew as much about the sport as any rower I have met. A successful economist, he had a touch of the poet too—"clock maker" is not half bad as metaphor. And, let's face it, his judgment was fair: at the time my rowing was a mess.

Although I felt as if my body were straight, I was actually twisting to the left during the drive. A visit to the chiropractor revealed the combination of an injury in a car accident and years of bad posture had left me with my left hip torqued slightly forward. Improvement would be not merely a matter of effort and concentration in the boat, but rather would require physical therapy, posture class, and a regime of stretching.

The coach, therefore, had snapped at me without offering a constructive clue. Yet when all is said and done he was indeed helpful, because he had first made me aware of a problem.

A seasoned editor once told me that a good writer can learn something even from "the most intemperate of reviewers," as he put it. Accordingly I did learn something from the coach's stinging verdict, and never again did I row with quite so little grace. But I didn't learn nearly as much as I might have from an understatement. I'll take a helping hand over an iron fist, any day.

We masters athletes—that is, those of us on the wrong side of thirty—are admittedly a touchy bunch. Touchy and toothy: we bleed easily and we bite back with gusto. Among coaches and officials, masters athletes have a reputation for sour grapes and well-thumbed copies of the rule book. No doubt there is something to the reputation. I have seen masters rowers throw tantrums at losing or kick up a fuss about the winning boat's alleged violations of the rules; as it happened, a charge without justification. Like Little League dads, masters athletes may well take competition far more seriously than do their younger counterparts.

No age, however, has a monopoly on vanity. Even a child would rather be told that, while his rowing is coming along nicely, he should pay more attention to getting his blades out of the water squared-up, than be told that his oars at the finish look like a pair of eggbeaters. A good coach practices the art of motivation by isolating an error, telling the athlete how to correct it, and then complimenting him on improvement. "That's it! Keep at it." Sweet words for the trainee.

Asking a coach to be a psychologist is asking a great deal. Since you might as well be hanged for a sheep as a lamb though, let us ask for one thing more. Let us ask that a coach pay as much attention to klutzes as to stars. Not many coaches in fact are so evenhanded, and who can blame them? An Olympian cuts a better figure than a clodhopper and a winning coach is more likely to get his contract renewed than is a humanitarian. Perhaps some coaches even feel that klutzes serve a useful purpose and should be left the way God made them: like wallflowers at a prom, klutzes keep everyone else on their toes. Once, for example, I overheard a sculler clucking over the clumsiness of some of the adults in the Learn to Row class which he had volunteered to coach. "Seeing them," he said, "I was really grateful to my parents for having forced me to do sports when I was a kid."

So the tyranny of the talented. In sports, King Knack reigns supreme. Too often is it considered acceptable to make fun of the ungifted. Childish behavior, but sports is generally the domain of the young. Since a coach represents maturity, she will want to do better. A coach has to be there for athletes who never did sports as a kid as well as for those who brought home the trophies. Not only does disdain for the ungainly pierce thin skins, but it breeds overconfidence: as if the race were to the swift. By contrast, consider the challenge of helping an athlete who doesn't get it right on the first try, or on the fifth, and consider the satisfaction of seeing her finally nail a technique. Consider too the sweet solidarity among those who acknowledge the dash of klutz that is probably in all of us.

One summer I rowed in a coxed four. Aside from me, who was nearing forty, the rowers were all in their twenties. One, a grad student in chemistry, ran marathons. A second, a law clerk, played semipro basketball in winter. A third, an engineering student, had done a tour of duty in the U.S. Rangers, and he had the close-cropped look and—judging by the martial arts exercises with which he warmed up—taste for a fight to match. In short, they were a tough lot, with athletic pedigrees running pages longer than mine.

They seemed formidable. The basketball player was a Hercules. He rowed starboard, and when he rowed his hardest, it was all the port rowers could do to keep the boat from veering to one side. He made me feel like a dentist's drill, sharp and thin and overspecialized. The marathoner, whom I sat behind, had lungs of steel. My stabbing gasps of air after each stroke seemed to profane the silence of his effortless work. As for the ex-soldier, he rowed stroke with the same precision with which he had parachuted from speeding airplanes. Once every few strokes I peeked at his oar and silently cursed my inability to keep to his good rhythm: quick finish, slow recovery, square-up early, crisp catch, powerful drive.

The guys were hard to keep up with, but I held my own. I owe it all to our coach. She was a big, good-humored woman who willingly squeezed herself into the coxswain's seat—necessary most days, since we couldn't find a regular cox. Strong and tough, fresh from the varsity crew herself, she worked us hard. We did power pieces and pyramids, practiced racing start after racing start, and rowed with our feet out of the stretcher to improve body control. We learned new drills with strange names like "cutting the cake," and learned that we had a long way to go before mastering old exercises like the pause drill (in which the rower pauses at various points during the recovery in order to check body position). We did many power pieces. I can still hear Coach calling out the strokes: "In three more strokes we'll build up over three strokes for a power ten. One, two, three: bu—i—ld one, b—u—i—ld two, b—u—i—l—d three. *Power ten!*" She worked us hard, but she had the voice of a songbird and the manner of a hen. The more she tried to sound like a drill sergeant, the more she sounded like a choirmaster. She was tough but self-deprecating, and I knew she was rooting for those who were not naturals.

Her best drill was one in which we rowed with closed eyes. We were not flying on automatic pilot but rowing with heightened senses, ears attuned to rhythm and body keen to every motion. Like a weight-lifting exercise in which you isolate one muscle, so the drill isolated the senses and gave them a workout while leaving the intellect in reserve. The theory was that the body would step in where the mind was locked out, with the result that we would end up rowing in sync, like one person instead of four. To encourage success, the coach held the drill back until the end of a practice, when we had worked through our rustiness. Still, I was skeptical.

I guess I'm always skeptical about letting go of the mind and trusting the body. In childhood I fussed before I let them take off the training wheels on my two-wheeler. As a teenager with a new driver's license, I hated starting a trip before plotting my course on a map. Today one of my favorite coaches is the silent coach: that is, the book. I'm a sports-book junkie. I devour anything on rowing or on conditioning. It's not that I distrust flesh-and-blood coaches, just that I need my training wheels. We intellectuals are convinced that the brain conquers all. So I was skeptical of rowing blind.

I ought to have had more faith. Coach's drill might have been designed for the unnatural athlete. By shutting my eyes I closed out my doubts. Forced to listen to my own body, I learned to my surprise that it could speak, and that what it said was yes. We would row together in harmony; yes, I would keep up with the other guys. In ten strokes we had achieved "swing," which is to rowing what the beat is to jazz. Swing is what harmony is to a chorus. Swing is all grooves and sockets, swing is the glide of a swallow and the stretching of a cat, swing is the sound of the ball as it spins across the felt and drops into the pocket. The four of us rowed as one, and I could not tell you where my hand ended and my oar began, or where my seat ended and the next began. We were not four individuals: we were a boat.

Sometimes the best way to get ahead is to put yourself in a coach's hands and to follow as faithfully as a blind man follows a Seeing Eye dog. You cannot say where it will lead, but it will take you someplace that you would not have found on your own. When I opened my eyes at the end of the drill that day, for example, the water looked as smooth and shiny as a new moon.

A good coach can erase the past; a good coach can invent the future. "Inspire me!" a coach once called out to a bunch of us, challenging us on a morning when we were sculling with less vigor than pensioners arranging bingo chips. I took his challenge, applying concentration and muscle and, by the end of the day's row, I did inspire him. Coach rewarded me with a compliment about how well I had been rowing lately. Let it be said: I was over forty, but I glowed like a grade-school kid who had just been sent to the head of the class. That day when I carried the shell on my head back to the boathouse, the shell felt light as a feather.

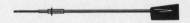

It is desirable therefore to have a colorful, poetic, perceptive, and caring coach, but none of these characteristics is essential. There are, however, three qualities that, it seems to me, no coach can do without.

First, a good coach must be an expert. He must know his sport thoroughly. He must know the secret, unforeseeable details, the things that seem simple and obvious once you learn them but which you would never have figured out on your own. I think, for example, of a coach I met one summer, a red-faced and pleasant man with a big laugh and a relaxed manner that belied his ability to cut right to the point. He came up in his launch beside my shell one morning and said to me that it was obvious to him, that I was rushing up the slide on my recovery. As a result, my rhythm was off and my stroke was short. Luckily I could break the habit easily. As I headed toward the catch, he said, I had merely to think about pulling myself up the slide by my toes. His advice worked. As soon as I followed it, the rhythm of my stroke improved. By slowing my pace I gained the time to add a few extra inches to the distance the boat as well as each oar traveled on each stroke, thereby helping me relax and making each stroke longer and more efficient. I myself would never have expected to find the secret of a good stroke in my toes, but the coach, the expert, knew better.

The second thing that every coach must be is a parent—not literally, that is, but metaphorically. Like a parent, he has to command respect and love and fear and obedience. He has to know that the athlete both models himself on him and wants to please him, the way a child does his father or mother. During practice, as the coach turns his head inspecting each athlete in turn, if he senses that nervousness is mixing with eagerness, if he sees fear and pride, if he hears crisp and constant sounds, then he knows that he is doing his job well.

Take my coach, who suggests that I run stadium stairs, "to build up aerobic endurance." I have always hated running stadium stairs, and am convinced, moreover, that the exercise will rip holes in my knee tendons. But it is my coach speaking. Just before sunup, a hazy summer morning finds me hauling myself up and down the steps of the university's football stadium. Coaches have a way of doing that to you. It turns out to be the single hottest morning of the year, already 72 degrees Fahrenheit with humidity over 80 percent. But I am not alone. The visitors stands across the field echo with the hammering sound of fifty junior high summer-campers running up and down their steps, egged on by—who else?—a coach. I am cheating, I suppose, by running up the thirty yard line, where there are fewer steps, but as I pant and strain and try not to trip, they seem more than enough to me. An hour later my lungs feel clean and pure, and I think how right the coach was.

The third quality of a good coach is by far the most important: he must master the art of sharing knowledge. He needs to render an athlete able not merely to mimic a certain skill or technique but to grab hold of it and make it his own. The coach gives the athlete the pieces but the athlete puts them together into a whole. My coach, for example, told me—more times than I wanted to hear—that I was burying the blades on my drive and slowing the boat. I am grateful that he kept after me, but I am even more grateful that he knew when to leave me alone so that I could experiment and flail and fail until slowly, slowly, I made things click. Only when you feel for yourself how much faster the boat moves when it is not being held back by blades stuck deep in the water, only then will you know why the blades should be shallow. It will become second nature, and forever afterward you'll make an effort not to bury them. Then and only then will you understand the coach.

What you might not understand though—I don't mind admitting that I don't understand—is just how a coach manages to turn his words into your instincts or mine. It is a knack and, I am sure, a mystery. I am reminded of an American archaeologist I once knew as a student in Greece. He was venerable and elderly, a wisp of a man who had survived the rigors of a concentration camp, where the Nazis had sent him because of his ties to the Greek resistance. He was very shy and very tall, tall enough no doubt to have a direct line to Olympus. In any case, he seemed to carry with him every secret there was to know about the ruins of the Greek countryside and, now and then, he generously divulged one to us students. But his words always bore the mystery of grace and the challenge of election. Take, for instance, his advice as to how to find an ancient road: "You will feel the road under your feet." I loved the thought, a riddle which quickly acquired the status of maxim. I loved even more the walks to ancient sites in the hills around Athens that he sometimes led us on. If I, for one, could never have found an ancient road without a neon sign pointing the way, it made little difference. Somehow one or two of my fellow students unwrapped the enigma and did discover ancient roads of their own. The old archaeologist kindled a fire in their hearts that burned without fuel.

I don't know how he did it, any more than I know how a coach does it when he turns the dross of unformed talent into gold medals. In my more academic moments I am tempted to scare up a word like *hierophant:* a priest who showed sacred symbols of eternal life to followers of ancient Greek religion, thereby initiating them into the ranks of the blessed. But happily, a simple word best describes the third and most important quality of a coach, the ability to show you something clearly enough that you understand it. That word is *teacher.*

To teach, says *Webster's* is "to show or help to learn how to do something." This time, etymology is enlightening. "Teach" comes from a similar Old English root as "token," a root whose basic sense is to show or demonstrate. A good teacher or a good coach makes his lesson so lively that he might be giving you a token, a tangible symbol that you can hold in your hand, like an oar: something that you can get to know, something that you can keep. So knowledge passes from teacher to pupil, from coach to athlete.

Yet a coach is not simply a teacher, at least not a

teacher as found in a modern university. For one thing, a coach's pedagogical goal is practical wisdom, while a college teacher usually imparts theoretical understanding. The coach teaches the right way to do something, while the college teacher offers the tools to evaluate something in many different ways. To return to the archaeologist's metaphor, the coach shows you the ancient road, while the college teacher shows you how to know when you have found a road yourself.

For another thing, a college teacher has a more limited portfolio than a coach. College teachers pass on knowledge too, and aim at being experts, but parenthood is something that they tend to keep at arm's length. A college teacher is reluctant to stand as an example to the students, and dishing out advice is risky business. A great teacher, to be sure, forces students to examine the comfortable but unexamined underpinnings of their souls, but few of us are great teachers. Often today's teacher is more like a milkman, dropping off knowledge without waking anyone up, just as a milkman used to drop off bottles on the doorstep in the predawn hours. Not so a coach. Like a guide in the wilderness, a coach must keep close to his followers. To be useful, he has to get in their way.

Nor can a coach adopt the airy detachment of many a lecturer, to take a third point. No teacher risks a pink slip if her students fail, say, to get into Harvard medical school, so often a scholar can take it or leave it when it comes to the students' learning their lessons. Coaches, by contrast, are judged by the success of their athletes. To succeed, coaching must be intimate and intense. It concerns flesh and blood, body as well as mind. Teaching calculus or the War of the Roses might not require passion but forging a winning team does.

So speaks the old hand at teaching. I am battle-scarred, no doubt, but not pessimistic: I simply marvel at the possibilities of expanding the academic mind if practical wisdom and passion were to become as ingrained in it as they are in coaching, and if teachers had as much a stake in their students' success as coaches do in their athletes'. If students were to adopt the discipline and respect of athletes, and if teachers were to adopt the intensity and care as well as the expertise of a coach—if teachers were again to become mentors and not merely conveyors of knowledge—then the classroom would be a different place.

In the meantime, I am grateful to have rowed across the water under watchful eyes and in earshot of a patient voice.

Since its emergence as a modern sport in the nineteenth century, rowing has been blessed with great coaches. Gentlemen and professionals, pragmatists and visionaries, generals and prophets, mentors and wizards, engineers and bards, autocrats and comrades—many characters have inspired crews to row smarter or harder or faster.

An expert could compile a complex typology of coaching and its evolution into different styles. To my amateur eye, rowing coaches tend toward one of two poles: either they are analysts or intuitives. Analysts emphasize science, intuitives trust nature; analysts pay attention to details, intuitives stress the big picture; analysts employ a factual approach, intuitives reach for inspiration. The history of modern rowing offers many examples of each type of coach—two of the earliest and best are Charles Courtney, for the analysts; and Steve Fairbairn, for the intuitives. Courtney began coaching in the 1880s; Fairbairn, a generation younger, coached in the early twentieth century. Courtney was an American for whom rowing was a craft; a moral craft, to be sure, but nonetheless a matter of diagrams and photographs and strict training. Fairbairn, an Australian whose family had, for generations, sent its sons to Jesus College, Cambridge, saw rowing as metaphysics. Fairbairn broke with the contemporary emphasis on body posture and made bladework the essence of rowing; the body would take care of itself. The result was fluid, natural, and successful. Fairbairn won races and converts; his style spread first in England, then Germany and beyond. His writings are elegant, aphoristic, oracular. "Loose and easy, lazy and long" is one of his many quotable phrases as well as a summation of his principles. With his circle of disciples, Fairbairn resembled a philosopher as much as a coach.

It would be a privilege to have been trained by either man, but forced to choose I would prefer Fairbairn and his spirituality. Yet it is Courtney whom I feel that I know. A carpenter by trade and a self-taught rower, Courtney represents democracy in action. His curious career makes him the patron saint of second chances. Then there is the accident of geography.

Cayuga Lake probably saw its greatest rower in Courtney (1849–1920). He was born and died in the tiny town of Union Springs, at the lake's northern end. He spent over thirty years at its southern end, coaching Cornell crews. For two seasons, in 1895 and 1896, Courtney coached in the very boathouse from which I row.

I imagine him as he looks in turn-of-the-century pictures, with the stern eyes of a Victorian and the girth of a paterfamilias. Coach Courtney garnered a reputation as an authoritarian and a moralist. He dismissed varsity rowers not merely for drinking or smoking or cheating on an exam, but even for eating strawberry shortcake before a race. Courtney was a scientist too. He pioneered the use of machines and photographs to monitor his rowers' technique. He invented an improved version of the sliding seat. Not to be slowed by the upstate winters, Courtney is said to have had the Cayuga Inlet dynamited come March, an effective if illegal way to break up the ice; he is said to have given the fish to the police chief. Courtney's single-mindedness paid off in a superb record of wins and losses, including an undefeated stretch from 1885 to 1892. Revered by his rowers as the Old Man, Courtney appears every inch the coach as disciplinarian and analyst, not a bit the coach as poet; until, that is, his earlier career comes into consideration. Then an element of wildness slips into sight.

Photos from the 1870s of the young Courtney show him cutting a figure out of Eakins, looking lean and skillful in a boat. In those days he was a celebrated sculler who counted among his achievements an international single sculling championship won at Philadelphia in 1876 before a million spectators. That was as an amateur, when he won every race; when he turned professional Courtney did not fare as well. The professional rowing circuit was as popular in the 1870s and 1880s as the professional tennis circuit is today. Courtney aimed for its apex but he was dogged by scandal instead. In their first meeting, Courtney lost narrowly to the great Canadian sculler Ned Hanlan. He dropped out of one race in humiliation, because of sun poisoning, before the president and much of his cabinet and Congress; he dropped out of another because someone slipped him a mickey. His worst forfeit though came when his scull was mysteriously sawed in half just before his rematch with Hanlan. His detractors claimed that Courtney had arranged for the sawing rather than risk a second defeat; his supporters blamed Hanlan's men. A small-town boy, Courtney defended himself as the victim of the city slickers who were in the business of fixing races in the Gilded Age. Perhaps he had indeed been gulled or perhaps he had turned a blind eye to temptation or perhaps he had succumbed to it.

Coaching gave him a second chance. When Courtney was hired as a college coach in 1883 he was thirty-four. Editorialists fumed about letting the likes of him loose on impressionable youth. As a stern mentor Courtney proved them wrong, becoming in the process "the first great American pro crew coach," as historian Ronald Smith calls him. He might have added that Courtney also became the latest in the line of heroes, going back to Gilgamesh, who learned painful wisdom as they grew older and, in the process, became teachers.

4

The Greeks

They were good boys, my comrades, they didn't call out
From fatigue or thirst or frost,
They bore up like trees and waves
That accept the wind and the rain
Accept the night and the sun
Never changing amidst change.
They were good boys, whole days
They sweated at the oar with lowered eyes
Breathing in rhythm
And their blood turned their skin red in obedience.

—GEORGE SEFERIS, *Mythistorema 4* (My transaltion)

I am rowing toward the past. I am trying to squeeze out
of each stroke a better image of myself, and I am trying to enlist the ghosts of history to help power the
oars. I want them as friends, as comrades, as partners, as
ancestors.

I would, if I could, rewrite my personal history. I would
like to have been one of those hail-fellow-well-met, slap-
on-the-back guys who rowed crew in college. I might not
have gotten beyond second boat, it is true, but that would
only have made my tales grow taller in later years. I would
have cultivated metaphors comparing life to sports, partic-

ularly to seat races: contests in which a coach chooses his top rowers by comparing the results obtained when person A rows in a given seat with the results obtained with person B rowing in that same seat. I would be insufferable and satisfied.

Or would I? In college I was an editor on the student daily. I was far too driven by books and far too ambitious a journalist to have time for much else. To the extent I noticed the existence of crew at all, I saw only what appeared to be a cult of big-boned acolytes who rose at dawn. Had I been then who I am now, I would have given my eyeteeth to have rowed crew in college; put me in the tenth boat, I would still have been overjoyed. In retrospect though, the consequences of such a change would have been so momentous—a change substituting sunshine for gloom, balance for volatility, orange juice for coffee, hero-worship of the Rowin' Kellys for the Writin' Woodwards (Bob and C. Vann)—that imagining the possibility is simply out of court. Had I been a rower then I might not be a writer today.

Deferring my start as a rower was good for my profession, but not for my body. Learning a sport at forty is not like learning a sport at fourteen. Supple and casual, the teenager laughs off a beginner's mistakes and has all the time in the world to correct them. The forty-year-old body is as brittle as the mind is intense. Learning new skills comes more slowly. Feeling like a freshman again goes against the grain of professional pride. The fourteen-year-old can look forward to increasing strength and to the glory of competition at the elite level. The masters athlete, by contrast, has to fight off decay and he can count on popular indifference. The forty-year-old novice is the forgotten man of athletics, part dreamer and part fool, part plugger and part misfit. That is why I like the Greeks.

Ancient Greece: now there was a place for a rower. With its indented coastline, its bays and coves, its nearly 1,500 islands, Greece is practically one big ship. Its ancient seafarers are legendary, from Odysseus to Jason. His Argonauts had Orpheus as coxswain and Hercules in the "engine room"—the seats amid ships where the coach places his strongest rowers—where Hercules rowed so hard that he eventually snapped his oar in half. A poet describes the power of the rowers of the *Argo:*

> So to the lyre of Orpheus they struck with their
>   oars
> The furious water of the sea, and the surge broke
>   into waves.
> Here and there the dark brine gushed with foam,
>   Roaring terribly through the strength of the
>   mighty men. (My translation)

The Greeks perfected, perhaps invented, the trireme: a sleek, three-decked wooden warship rowed by 170 oarsmen and armed with a bronze ram at its bow. They were crammed into a ship only about 120 feet long, about twelve feet high, and about eight-and-a-half feet above the waterline. In Greece, fast ships were christened *Torch-Bearer* or *Victory* or the like; legendary oarsman had nicknames like Sparwood or Pullerman; poets gushed about rowers who plowed furrows in the choppy sea. A place for a rower; or was it?

The Greeks did a lot of rowing, and yet they were not in love with their oars the way an American, say, is in love with his automobile. Athens, Rhodes, Corinth, Corfu were the greatest sea powers among the city-states. The best-documented of them is Athens, a place where every boy learned to row but few adults rowed unless they had to. Rowing was back-breaking work. And dangerous. And déclassé. Poor Greeks dreamt not of rowing boats but of racing horses, just as working people today dream not of Chevrolets but Porsches. Consider that icon of western art, the Parthenon. It was built about 2,500 years ago, in the era (the fifth-century B.C.) when Athens ruled the seas. The ordinary Athenian seaman had an extraordinary say in his government, the first democracy in history. Yet the sculpture that runs in bands around the colonnades of the Parthenon depicts not rowers or ships, but cavalrymen and their horses. Imagine a union hall today decorated with photographs not of steelworkers and stevedores but of famous football players and boxers driving Corvettes and Trans-Ams.

I like rowing because I like old things, and rowing is a very old thing, as old as the pyramids. The ancient Egyptians held regattas on the Nile. They celebrated rowers in wall paintings and carved reliefs. Pharaoh did not disdain the sport. An inscribed stone found near the Sphinx, for example, praises the rowing prowess of Pharaoh Amenhotep II, who lived nearly 1,500 years before Christ. The Egyptians liked rowing so much that they even paid it the compliment of using it in a tasteful erotic fantasy, a tale of twenty pretty girls rowing back and forth across a lake at the palace, wielding gold-plated, ebony oars and wearing only nets made of pearls instead of clothes. The scene is reminiscent of the Bible and of Shakespeare. Consider, first, this description from Ezekiel of the galleys of Tyre:

Of the oaks of Bashan have they made thy oars;
the company of the Ashurites have made thy
benches of ivory, brought out of the isles of Kittim. (Ezekiel 27:6)

Now, here is Shakespeare's portrait of Cleopatra on her galley, seducing Mark Antony:

The barge she sat in, like a burnish'd throne,
Burn'd on the water: the poop was beaten gold;
Purple the sails, and so perfumed that
The winds were love-sick with them; the oars
    were silver,

Which to the tune of flutes kept stroke and made
The water which they beat to follow faster,
As amorous of their strokes.

(Antony and Cleopatra, II, ii)

The Romans enjoyed boat races and also mock naval battles. The emperor Augustus, for example, established an
annual regatta to celebrate his victory at sea over Antony
and Cleopatra at the Battle of Actium in 31 B.C. The
Greeks were less enamored of boat races, but boats are
expensive and Greece has always been poor. The Romans
were rich.

In his epic poem, the *Aeneid* (19 B.C.), the Latin poet
Virgil describes a regatta with a fan's eye and a poet's ear.
As a rower, I nod in agreement at some of the details. I
feel that I could have been part of Virgil's sketch, for
instance, of the nervous scene at the starting line. The
poet notices the *intenta* (taut) arms of the *intenti* (intent)
oarsmen as they wait for the signal to go, while he imag-
ines a mix of *pavor pulsans* ("pounding fear") and *laudumque
arrecta cupido* ("the aroused desire for glory") draining their
hearts. He writes:

The oarsmen are crowned with poplar leaves,
Their young shoulders shine brightly, anointed
   with oil.
They take their seats on the benches, arms taut on
   the oars,
Intent they await the signal while pounding fear

And the aroused desire for glory drain their
  bounding hearts. (My translation)

Then the trumpet sounds and the boats are off, faster and
more powerful than chariots. The crowd roars.

Virgil goes on to report the particulars of the race. I
like the way he captures the straining of a crew that has
fallen behind as it tries to take back, if not first place, then
at least its honor. The rowers bend forward on each stroke
certamine summo ("with the height of striving"), driving the
boat *vastis ictibus* ("with enormous strokes") while *creber
anhelitus artus aridaque ora quatit* ("thick breathing shakes
their limbs and parched mouths") and *sudor fluit undique
rivis* ("sweat flows in streams everywhere"). You can almost
hear their collective breath hissing out in the asonance of
anhelitus artus aridaque ora. Virgil writes:

They bend forward with the height of striving;
The bronze-tipped ship trembles at the enormous
  strokes
And the ocean floor is drawn up from beneath
  them. Then thick breathing
Shakes their limbs and parched mouths; sweat
  flows in streams everywhere. (My translation)

After almost pulling off an upset, the crew comes in second.

In Greece rowing was not primarily a sport but a way
of war. Naval commanders organized regattas to keep

crews in fighting trim. Alexander the Great, for instance, organized a naval regatta on the Tigris River at Babylon. Ironically, Alexander had made his mark not at sea but as a cavalry commander. Not only was Alexander no rower, he did not even know how to swim.

Regattas were part of a few Greek athletic festivals, for example, the Great Panathenaic Festival, held once every fifth year in Athens, which was Greece's leading maritime state. Only Athenian citizens could participate. They were divided into ten teams, which took part in a boat race, probably for triremes. The winning team got a cash prize, three bulls, and two hundred free meals; the second-place team took home a smaller cash prize and two bulls.

Not bad, but not in a league with the rewards of an ancient Olympic champion, who was fed for life at public expense and who sometimes parlayed athletic success into political office. Rowing would not have been the champion's sport, however, for there was no rowing at the ancient Olympic Games, nor at most of the other major Greek athletic competitions. Indeed, although the names of many ancient athletic victors have survived, not a single one is a rowing champion. Why was rowing so invisible a sport? Sports reflect the society that plays them.

Ancient Greece was a rugged place, in which a man who did not fight for his country did not have a full share of honor. Traditionally, war in Greece had been a rich man's game, or at least a game that excluded the many men who had difficulty making ends meet. Unlike their more prosperous neighbors, dirt-poor farmers or fisher-

men or goatherds or shoemakers did not march off to battle to the sound of the flute-player nor march back to
wreaths and oratorical tributes. They could not afford an
infantryman's armor or servant or time to train, much less
afford a cavalryman's horse. When the trireme came into
prominence around 500 B.C., however, and the state introduced pay for rowers, poor men could furnish the one
thing an oarsman needed: a strong back. So they volunteered for a few months' service each year during the summer doldrums on the Greek farm and they went to sea.
They saw the world and they won their honor.

The view from the deck of a trireme as a rower pulled
his oar was remarkable. He saw 170 men moving as one,
maintaining "the regular dip of all the oars together," as
the playwright Aeschylus calls it. It was a community
effort and a political education. Having learned that
poverty was no bar to prowess, the rowers demanded their
share of political power back on shore. They could get
that power because, while the rowers of Athens were poor,
most of them were free men. It is true that slaves were
sometimes used as rowers when extra manpower was
needed, and mercenaries were common, but the core of
Athens' rowers was made up of Athenian citizens.

It is a far cry from the picture of an ancient warship
that sticks in many people's minds: the galley scene from
the film *Ben-Hur*. In that 1959 movie epic, Charlton Heston played Judah Ben-Hur, a Jew who was condemned to
slavery on a Roman galley. Metro-Goldwyn-Mayer
depicted his experience in detail, in close-up scenes shot

on reconstructed galleys docked off the Italian coast. (Ship models in a tank in Hollywood were used for a panorama of the battle.) Although there are many similarities between a Roman galley and Greek trireme, there are important differences in architecture and outfitting and personnel. As a galley slave, Ben-Hur labored under terrible conditions far different from a trireme. Along with the other rowers, all of them slaves too, he was chained by his ankles to a bench below deck. There he was forced to do back-breaking work to an ever-faster tempo marked by a drum-beating *hortator* (literally, "encourager"). As a slave, Ben-Hur lost even his name, having to be called instead Number Forty-One.

Since it is the movies, everything works out in the end for Ben-Hur. He survives a shipwreck and saves his commander too, and he is rewarded with wealth, honor, and affection in Rome. Athenian rowers did not enjoy quite so happy endings, in spite of their political success. Yet the free rowers of Athens received salaries and, on occasion, the slaves were rewarded with freedom, so they did make good in their own way. The film is more accurate about two other realities of ancient warships, whether Roman or Greek.

First, war galleys were dangerous. In a battle with a pirate fleet, Ben-Hur and his fellow slaves watched helplessly in their chains as an enemy ship raced toward them, bent on ramming. (Ben-Hur is unchained at the eleventh hour.) Athenian rowers too risked being rammed. Having no chains they could swim free but sometimes they ended up clinging to the debris of the wreckage until another ship could come to save them. After a battle in 406 B.C. a storm blew up and prevented the Athenian commanders from rescuing the shipwrecked. About 5,000 men drowned—and Athens had *won* that battle!

Second, rowing was hard work. Charlton Heston remembered in his book *In the Arena: An Autobiography* the experience of filming the galley scenes as having to "pull that damned oar . . . I put in my time in chains as Number Forty-One in the galley." In his journal of the making of *Ben-Hur* (from his book *The Actor's Life*) he recorded, for September 30, 1959: "In terms of pure physical effort, today was probably as hard as I've ever worked in any part. I spent the morning rowing, including the change of speeds Arrius [the Roman commander] tests Judah with. A real bone-breaker."

Nor was rowing always stimulating. Heston's journal for November 24, 1959 states: "That beard gets pretty boring after a day or two straight. So does the rowing. I think I pulled my last oar today, though. Everything else we have left in that sequence is after the galley is rammed."

Hard and dangerous and monotonous the rowing life may have been in the ancient Mediterranean, but the crews of the triremes gave Athens its sea power. Their proudest moment came in 480 B.C. when, off their own coast near the island of Salamis, they smashed an invasion fleet sent by the greatest empire of the day, Persia. The next seventy-five years witnessed the great age of Athenian sea power. Not coincidentally, they also marked the flowering of Athenian democracy. The wealthier classes of Athens who manned the infantry and the cavalry were forced to acknowledge the military importance of the rowers and to make political concessions. The wealthy made financial concessions too, which were fairly painless so long as the Athenian fleet collected tribute around the Aegean. One contemporary Greek author (his name has not survived) gives grudging praise to the justice of democracy: "It is right that the poor and the common people there [in Athens] have more than the well-born and the wealthy because it is the people who row the ships and furnish power to the city, and it is the helmsmen and the time-keepers and the pursers and the lookouts and the shipwrights—they are the ones who furnish power to the city more than the infantrymen and the well-born and the good men." (My translation)

In the work of Thucydides, the great historian of Athens' struggle with Sparta (the Peloponnesian War, 431–404 B.C.), the rowers come off as professional, disciplined, and self-confident. They moved with a precision and flair that turned ordinary maneuvers into showpieces. Even when outnumbered they rowed circles around the enemy—literally. For example, consider this engagement in 429 B.C. in the Gulf of Corinth. A Peloponnesian fleet of forty-seven ships outnumbered an Athenian fleet of only twenty ships, but the Athenian ships were faster and better outfitted for sea battle. The Peloponnesians tried, in effect, a quarterback sneak: they would block an Athenian rush and then have their best ships break out and attack the enemy. They underrated their opponent, however. The Athenian commander, Phormio, knew every trick in the playbook, and his men were pros. Thucydides describes the battle as follows:

> The Peloponnesians arranged their ships in as big a circle as they could—bows outward, sterns inward—without leaving the enemy space to row through. They also placed inside the circle the small craft that had accompanied them and the five fastest-rowing ships, so that, standing by a short distance away, they could row out if the enemy approached anywhere. The Athenians, arranged in single file, kept rowing around them in a circle and hemming them into a narrow space, rowing right next to them. Phormio [the Athenian commander] had prearranged with his men, however, not to attack until he gave the signal. For he hoped that the enemy would not remain in order, as foot-soldiers would have on land, but that the ships would fall upon each other and the small craft add to the confusion; if, moreover, the breeze should blow up from the gulf, which Phormio was awaiting as he rowed round and which usually came around dawn, the enemy would lose their composure in no time at all. Phormio thought that the initiative was his to take whenever he wished. As the breeze began to blow and the ships, already in a narrow space, were thrown into confusion both by the wind

and the small craft, ship fell upon ship and they tried to push them apart with poles. The Peloponnesian rowers employed such cries and warnings and abuse of each other that they paid no heed to the commands or the time-keepers, and since they were inexperienced they were unable to keep the blades clear of the rough water, and so they rendered the ships less obedient to the captains. At that crucial moment Phormio gave the signal. The Athenians fell upon the Peloponnesians; first they sank one of the commanders' ships and then they destroyed whichever of the others they came upon. In the ensuing confusion the enemy did not fight but fled instead to Patras and Dyme in Achaea. The Athenians pursued them and, after capturing twelve ships and picking up most of the men who had been on them, they sailed off to Molykreon. The Athenians set up a trophy on Rhion, dedicated a ship to Poseidon, and returned to Naupactus. (My translation)

Thucydides offers an almost poetic description of the Athenian fleet in his account of the Sicilian Expedition as it pushed off from the docks on a day in June. In 415, an Athenian fleet of over one hundred triremes rowed out from Piraeus, the port of Athens. The aim was nothing less than conquering the island of Sicily; hence the term, Sicilian Expedition. As Thucydides describes the scene, a huge crowd came down to the port to see the ships off.

They cheered, they wept, and they gawked—understandably, because the best crews had been recruited, best equipment provided; everything was in top shape; and everyone was risking his life on so long and ambitious a journey. The rowers had arrived at dawn to take their seats onboard. When all was finally ready, the departure made a gorgeous sight. Thucydides writes:

> When the ships were manned and everything that they were going to take with them had been put on board, a trumpet gave a signal for silence. A herald made the customary prayers before departure—but for the whole force rather than ship by ship. Wine bowls were filled and then representatives of the troops onboard and the commanders poured libations from gold and silver cups. And the rest of the crowd on the shore, both citizens and all others who were supporters of Athens, joined in the prayers. When they had sung the paean and completed the libations they set off. They sailed at first in single column and then they held a race as far as the island of Aegina. (My translation)

It was part pep rally, part religious ceremony, part regatta.

It was not, however, something to everyone's taste. Wealthy Athenians recognized the military and political power of the rowers, but they drew the line when it came to recognizing the equality of the rowers where that equality pinched the ego most tightly—on the playing field. Glory belonged to the aristocrats who raced horses and trained for running and wrestling.

Many a scholar today would agree, arguing that the Athenian oarsman felt less than a full man even about his military service. Unlike an infantryman the oarsman did not carry weapons, and unlike a cavalryman on his mount, he faced backward on the rowing bench. Yes, the poor boys who rowed the ships did not write memoirs or commission monuments, but if we could only hear their voices, just imagine what they might say.

Consider one of the few ancient representations of oarsmen, the so-called Lenormant Relief, a sculpture discovered in 1859 and now on display in the Acropolis Museum in Athens. Only preserved in part, the relief depicts a trireme under oar. Art historians date the relief to about 400 B.C. Its purpose is unclear, but it may well be one of the rare monuments to the Athenian fleet.

The surviving stone shows only seven oarsmen in profile, but these seven speak volumes about the 170 rowers on each ship. Not only does the sculptor reveal each man's hard work in his straining muscles, bent back, and outstretched arms hanging on the oar, but he takes the trouble to note individual variations in style. The seven men work as a unit. Each one has reached the same phase of the stroke cycle: having made the catch he has begun pulling through the drive. Idiosyncrasies of style nonetheless stand out. One rower, for instance, is getting the maximum out of his back, another is letting his shoulders lean forward; one rower is locking his elbows, another bending them slightly; one rower is tired, another looks like he is just warming up.

These are hard-working boys. The sculptor takes them and their craft seriously. His work reveals humanity and humor, skill and pride. I don't believe these oarsmen yielded an inch to land fighters when it came to honor, nor when it came to courage, for anyone who risked the threat of being rammed at sea could hold his head high back on land.

Could they but speak, the Athenian rowers would voice pride and confidence. Their speech does not survive, but their cheer does: *Ruppapai!* I imagine that cheer echoing in response to the rowing master's call, a call that perhaps did not differ greatly from the steersman's call to the Nile boatmen in the words of a nineteenth-century song: "My sons, you are men, row away stoutly."

Ruppapai! The cheer sounded on Athenian warships with such fierce names as the *Lion,* the *Spear,* the *Achilles,* the *Hardy,* the *Prowess,* or the *Courageous.* The oarsmen deserved all the honor the names imply.

Largely overlooked at the great athletic games of Greece, largely unsung in the art and literature that celebrated them but proud and diligent nonetheless, the ancient rower has something in common with today's masters athlete. In our own small way, perhaps we masters athletes have something to learn too from the risks the Greeks took.

Sculling is dangerous. To step into any boat is to take a risk, and far more so to step into a fragile, unstable vessel and then exercise to the point of exhaustion. Yet the hazards often escape our attention. The elegance of the glide through the water, the gentleness of the sculler's bodily motion—which is of far lower impact than jogging—the genteel associations of oars, Harvard and Henley, not Madison Square Garden or the Colosseum, lull us. We forget that where there is guts there is usually blood.

Coaches remind us. They show us safety videos, send out launches to accompany novices, administer swim tests, tell us to carry life jackets and water bottles on our boats. They teach us what to do if the boat flips, how to float with an oar or by holding on to an overturned shell. Often they teach these lessons vividly.

When once I spent a week at a sculling camp in New England, for example, flipping the scull was, as it were, the price of admission. Flipping was the first thing we did in our first class on our first day. Taking a single scull out from the dock and flipping it was a cinch and, in the cold waters of a northern lake in summer, a tonic. Getting back into the upright boat was the tricky part. It took several tries before I got the oars balanced properly and before my arms and hands got just the right purchase on the hull to pull myself up and in without tipping, or damaging, the boat.

Not that I was entirely unfamiliar with the art of flipping. We had no formal lessons in flipping in my club, but we did have the *Ariadne*. It was a heavy, mold-made fiberglass shell which had been left to the club by a former member, who had had it custom made. It suited his big frame—he weighed 225 pounds. When most people rowed the *Ariadne,* however, it sat high and unstable in the water, which was precisely why the coach insisted that beginners row at least fifty miles in it. He knew that most rowers would find the boat unstable and so would flip it willy-nilly and, one hoped, would learn to recover from a flip. Tough love.

I flipped the *Ariadne* my second time out in it. It was, fortunately, a summer afternoon. The water was warm, and I had just completed a good, long row: no fun to flip first and then face several miles of rowing in wet clothes. I had been trying to back into the dock, a neat maneuver, and one that saved me the trouble of rowing past the dock, turning, and rowing back to the dock. The disadvantage of backing is that it makes a boat much less stable than does rowing, especially when the boat is unstable to begin with and when the rower is inexperienced. I tipped the boat and went down. The fall, the wetness, the tangle of arms and legs, the blue submarine light all shocked me. I wiggled out from under the shell, shot up to the surface to gasp a breath of air, and cursed. I cursed loudly, though to no one in particular, for there wasn't a soul around the boathouse. My ego was glad that no one had seen my misstep, although it would certainly have been safer had someone been there to help me in case I had gotten into deeper trouble. As it was, I was close enough to shore to pull myself onto the dock and pull the boat in behind me.

My next flip was dramatic. It took place at dockside again, this time, upon my setting out. I had graduated to a racing shell which I was rowing for only the second time. It was early on a sunny summer morning. I was proud of the strides I had made in technique, and rightly so, but it turned out that I had paid insufficient attention to a small but serious matter: getting into the boat. When stepping into a single scull, the sculler uses one hand to hold onto the dock and the other hand to hold onto the oars, whose handles he brings together over the keel. An advanced sculler will step in and push off gracefully in one motion; a beginner will sit down in the boat first and only then push off. In either case, as he steps into the boat the sculler must hold both handles at once; otherwise the boat will lose its balance and tip. I forgot this last detail and let go of the handles momentarily. The boat did an instant somersault and threw me into the water of the creek.

The boathouse was bustling with business that morning. Two rowers ran down to the dock to help. I was already pulling myself back onto the wooden planks of the dock, and was ready to fish the boat in. I brushed off all concerns, and fully intended to get back in the boat and row, not deigning to notice the soaked condition of my clothes. The boathouse manager, who was there, might have stopped me, but he didn't have to: the boat stopped me. As we looked at the shell, we could see that during the flip a piece of the washbox (a wooden structure protecting the cockpit) had broken off. I could see, in fact, that I had accidentally broken it with a flailing limb or perhaps my bum. The damage turned out to be minor, but the boat had to go up on slings ashore until the manager could take a good look at it. I suppose I could have put my ego on slings too, but I put it back to work. Since I happened to have a change of workout clothes in my car, I resuited. The *Ariadne* was available, so I went out sculling in it. This time I remembered to hold both oars as I got into the boat.

It has been a while since I felt unstable enough in a scull to feel in danger of flipping, but then I have long since given up doing anything in a scull that might court danger. Even the merest hint of a first date with danger makes me head back to the dock. Risk lost its romance when I experienced a part of rowing history I could happily have forgone: I got rammed.

It was the end of a long, hot day in late August. Psychologically it was the longest day of the year, in fact, for it was the first day of classes at the start of a new academic calendar, the end of summer vacation. I had taught both in the morning and the afternoon. In the early morning I had been too busy with class preparation to go sculling, but at the day's end I decided to reward myself with a good, hard workout. Around 5:00 P.M. I put a single in the water and pushed off from the dock.

Now it was late August, and this was no 5:00 P.M. of shadows and cool breezes. It must have been ninety degrees out, humid, and still. I was wearing a baseball cap and I had a water bottle but, 6:00 A.M. sculler that I usually am, I was not prepared for the blazing summer afternoon. Shoreline reflections were not where I was used to seeing them. My pacing, right for the early morning, was too intense for the afternoon heat. I was sweaty and uncomfortable. By the time my bow poked out from under the bridge and I faced the last stretch of the inlet, I was bushed.

I was in good form nonetheless. Perhaps that was the problem, for had my sculling been clearly off, I might have paid more attention to the risks. I rowed slowly up to the head of the inlet. I kept in lane, staying close to the west side of the channel, well aware that the middle of the channel was reserved for boats heading in the other direction, back down the inlet. As I turned to check my course halfway to the end, I could see heat shimmering in the distance, but no boats. I thought I had a clear path to the finish. Confident that I was the only boat about, and tired in the heat, I grew lax about checking my course. The distance lengthened between each turn of my head: first it was every fourth stroke, then every seventh stroke, then every tenth stroke.

I heard them shouting before I saw them, and then I felt the impact. I vibrated as if from an electric jolt; I felt like a tuning fork, with my oars the two tines. A pair rowed by two novices had wandered off course and into me. The handle of the bow rower's port oar hit my back, while my starboard oar thumped her in the head. I was stunned and sore, but I was sitting still in my scull. They say that after a serious accident the mind, as a form of healing, forgets the horror of the actual collision. If that is true, then my accident was less than serious. Not only did all involved (including the boats) recover quickly, but I suffered no memory loss at all. I remember everything, from the realization that we were going to hit each other, to the crash, to my insistence to the bowwoman that even though she felt all right she had suffered a head injury and had better get herself to see a doctor—she didn't, and turned out to be fine. I remember too the sudden relief that, hot out as it was, at least we were on the water where it was cool.

Neither boat had flipped, in fact, both were stable as could be. The pair had lost a piece of its washbox, but this was merely a cosmetic injury, and could easily be fixed. My single seemed to have suffered no damage at all. The three of us commiserated and fretted and swore and then rowed back—slowly, very slowly—the two miles to the boathouse. We passed plenty of other rowers as we headed down the inlet, but no one had seen our collision, and no one now gave us a second look. The boathouse was hopping when we got there, with people coming and going. They took the news of our crash in stride, which made me wonder if they were preoccupied or if crashes are more common than I had thought. In several years of rowing I had heard of a few collisions, but they had struck me as terrifying aberrations. Perhaps if we, or our equipment, had looked worse we would have received more attention.

On closer inspection at the dock, my single scull did look worse. The metal bar which held the adjustable footstretcher in place had cracked in half at the impact. It was an old boat, and the metal had probably been weak before the crash, but the ragged crack showed how much worse the accident might have been. All I suffered was a sore back and the time spent over the next week helping the boathouse manager repair the broken bar. What could it have been like to have been rammed in a galley?

Rowing was a blood sport in ancient Greece. The Greeks knew it. Consider an ancient gravestone in the National Archaeological Museum in Athens. At the top of the two-foot-high marble stone an inscription names the departed. He was Demokleides, son of Demetrios, an Athenian who died around 400 B.C. Demokleides was, it seems, a good-looking young man—well formed, curly haired, dreamy eyed—yet sadness hangs over him as it might over a hunchback. For one thing, the sculptor portrays Demok-leides sitting on the ground, knees raised, neck curled, head leaning on his right hand, right elbow resting on his right thigh. He holds his right knee with his left hand. He is almost in the fetal position. For another thing, Demok-leides is no heroic nude but, rather, is dressed in an ordinary robe. Its folds hang on the ground beside him. Behind him is a shield with a helmet on it, both resting on the ground.

As striking as Demokleides's posture is his size. The sculptor has rendered him in miniature, crowded into the upper right-hand corner of the gravestone. Most of the stone is taken up by what looks, at first sight, to be a large and empty hillside on which the departed is sitting. Only on first sight: as you approach the stone, and if you know a little about ancient technology, you realize that it is no hillside that dwarfs the seated figure but rather, a warship, its wooden prow and bronze ram visible in profile to the left of Demokleides. The bottom third of the stone was probably originally painted blue to show the sea.

So Demokleides died at sea, on a warship, perhaps in one of the great battles of the Peloponnesian War. Judging by his armor, he might have been a marine. In normal times, Athenian marines did little rowing, but when Demokleides died around 400 B.C., Athens was in crisis. The fleet needed every man it could get, so Demokleides is likely to have manned an oar, marine or not. To look at the gravestone of Demokleides, therefore, is to get a reminder that a rower in Athens risked a lot more than losing the victory wreath. His racing days might end with a 450-pound bronze ram smashing through the hull of his boat.

It is a long way from an ancient Greek galley to a modern rowing boat, even if a team of archaeologists and naval architects has recently reconstructed a full-scale, hypothetical Athenian trireme, called the *Olympias*. Rowed summers in Greece by volunteers (mainly college rowers, but also some masters) the *Olympias* makes a stirring sight among the pleasure crafts of the Aegean. It contributes mightily to scientific knowledge, yet I sometimes wonder if I don't feel closer to the ancients sitting in my single scull on the cold waters of Cayuga Lake than I might among the keen and sun-tanned rowers of the model.

Invisible comrades, the ancient Greeks speak to me about adversity. They knew adventure, they had fun, but they risked death, and they knew nothing of the leisure that we modern athletes enjoy. Born in poverty, they died in collective glory. They earned both money and political power on the rower's bench, but most important, they earned honor. If their names go unremembered, if no one cites them alongside Alexander or Socrates, then all the more poignant their testimony to the dictum that the truest heroism is the least sung.

"Prove thyself." So I think I hear the ancient oarsmen dare across the gap of centuries. I think I hear them say that the greatest victory is the victory over self-doubt.

5

The Race

A good swimmer
gets drowned;
A good rider
falls.

—ZEN PROVERB

Nothing about my first race in a single scull turned out as I had planned.

Well, one thing in fact did turn out as planned: I lost. Not that I had tried to lose. What I mean is that while my sculling was coming along nicely in practice, it was coming along slowly. I knew that I would not be competitive with the rowers who were likely to enter the race. So I did not sign up to win, but rather, to learn. Regatta day arrived, and I learned. I came, I rowed, I was conquered. As expected, but what I had not counted on was that my ego would get carved into three parts.

Ah, the best laid plans. It was my third season rowing,

and my maiden competitive voyage in a single scull. I had chosen a local regatta in a nearby town, a small friendly affair scheduled for a Saturday at the end of September. It was to be a head race, that is, a timed race in which boats start at about ten-second intervals and try to pass one another, rather than a sprint, in which all boats start at the same time and race side-by-side. The standard sprint course is straight and about a mile-and-a-half long; the head race course is usually about three miles, and it is typically narrow and winding. A head race, therefore, tests endurance and steering.

To prepare for the race, I put together a plan with a friend who is an experienced sculler. I would work out on the water four mornings a week, and keep my aerobic level up with brief workouts on land the other three days: when time permitted, swimming, otherwise skipping rope. The schedule was not the apex of dedication, which would have had me on the water every day, but it was an achievable goal. On Mondays I would row 2,000 meters at an 80 to 90 percent level of effort. On Wednesdays I would race all out down the Cayuga Inlet, a course of about two-and-a-half miles or 4,000 meters. On Fridays I would row three or four 500-meter pieces at a 100 percent effort. On Saturday or Sunday I would just go for a long row.

A month before the race the school year began. With it came teaching and committees and advisees and letters of recommendation and speakers visiting my university and me traveling to speak at other universities and dropping my daughter off at preschool and only one car between my wife and me. What had seemed like a reasonable schedule back in the summer now seemed as distant as a dog day afternoon at the swimming hole. The first week of September I cut back to three days a week of sculling. Then, three weeks before the race, an old lower-back injury began to flare up. A visit to the chiropractor brought the bad news that my back pain marked the beginning of what could turn out to be a nasty problem indeed, a slipped disk. Since I had caught it early, I could manage the problem with a series of exercises, but I would have to ease off on my sculling. I cut back to two days a week. Then, when I foolishly attempted to do some light weight lifting—to make up for the lost workout time on the water—I pulled a muscle in my right shoulder (another old injury inflamed). I went back to the chiropractor and alternated applications to my shoulder of ice pad and hot water bottle. When I tried to compensate for my temporary inability to pull hard by stepping up my jump rope regimen, to improve my aerobic capacity, I experienced a bad muscle cramp in my right calf. The chiropractor delivered the news: I might be able to race and I might not, but only if I rested completely. The regatta was only a week away, and I had only got in one practice during the previous week. So in the two weeks leading up to the regatta, I only had one practice in a scull; in the week before the race I had no practice at all.

Two days before the regatta I went back to the chiropractor. I could row, he said, if I felt up to it; only I knew how my body felt, and the final decision was up to me. How did my body feel? How does a deer feel strung up on a tree? A reasonable person would surely have decided to scratch the race. There would be other races, so better to heal and scull again another day. An unreasonable person, however, would have talked himself into a feat of will. He would have followed a risky recipe: take a dose of the need for immediate gratification, mix it well with the work ethic, pour the concoction into an hourglass-shaped vessel recalling the passage of time, and lace the brew with moral blackmail: "You're not afraid of racing, are you?"

The truth is, I was afraid. I was afraid of failing. I was afraid of looking foolish. I was afraid of getting up to the starting line and flipping the boat. I was afraid of being surpassed by other scullers in the club. Some of them were better scullers than I in spite of having less experience, which made me afraid of having to take my pride down a peg. I was afraid of thinking up a thousand reasons for putting off racing—reasons ranging from not being ready to having overtrained—and so letting the years go by until finally I would be racing in a shell equipped with a wheelchair. I was afraid of being afraid, terror having been an old teammate of mine since Little League days.

I had raced before. I had raced in eights, in fours, and in doubles. I had brought home medals and come into the finish line cursing, dead last. But I'd never raced in a single scull before. *Alone:* the word echoed in my imagination until I saw myself sculling on the river Styx at midnight on

Halloween, terror-stricken as the headless boatman closed in on me.

A chance meeting calmed me down. Shortly before the race I found myself giving a lecture in Indianapolis on what was, by coincidence, the first day of the world rowing championships. It was a fly-in-P.M., fly-out-A.M. visit, so my tight schedule did not allow me to see any events. But it turned out that I was spending the night in the same hotel as the American, British, and Australian national teams. The rowers were everywhere: in the lobby, on the mezzanine, in the elevator, in the hallways. They were tall and fit, but otherwise they were indistinguishable from other college students. At a major international competition I would have expected tension everywhere, but these kids looked confident and relaxed. No butterflies, no sleepless nights—they looked like they were having fun. The lobby of the hotel had the feel of a dorm room on a Friday night; only the pizza and beer were missing.

Back home, I smiled as I thought of those kids at the "Worlds," and I cheered when I read in the newspaper that the Americans had done better than expected, winning bronze, silver, and gold medals, including a victory in the prestigious men's eight. But as race day approached, my mood stiffened again. By night my subconscious lay telegraph lines through my brain which, all day long, clicked and clattered with a kind of Morse code of worry. Commands such as "Race—don't race—take a chance— play it safe—no excuses—why on earth do you care?" passed willy-nilly down my nerves and synapses. Worry tired me out; soon the bags under my eyes were bigger than my muscles.

The night before the race I drove down to the boat club to meet the other rowers and load the shells onto the trailer, a long, steel-frame truck with three layers for stacking boats. We were to bring to the race four single sculls, two doubles, a quad, and an eight. We took each boat down from its storage rack in the boathouse and placed it on a pair of wood-and-canvas slings. There, working in teams, we prepared each boat for transportation. Riggers extend from the shell and take up space on the trailer, so they have to be removed from each boat and transported separately. Anything in the boats that might come loose as a result of the vibrations of a trailer moving at fifty miles per hour has to be removed or tied down: seats, shoes, rowing meters. Then the boats have to be raised up and guided onto the trailer, where they are fastened with ropes and festooned with red flags at the bows as a warning to other drivers. The work is tedious, but monotonous work sometimes can make you forget how nervous you are. At least I did not sleep any worse that night than I had been sleeping all week.

At 6:30 the next morning another rower picked me up for the hour's drive to the race site. We headed north in the Finger Lakes region. I looked out from the passenger seat on the roadside, whose sights tumbled onto my drowsy consciousness like oracle bones onto the Chinese earth, obscure omens of the day ahead. Early-autumn wildflowers, purple and yellow, stood out against a background of empty fields and gray horizon. A drizzle started and stopped but the clouds did not clear. As we pulled into the regatta town, a dull mill town, we caught sight of the river. It was calm, as flat as a dead man's heartbeat. The omens were now clear. It was going to be an old penny of a day, dull and mediocre but precise in its value. A shy day, hesitant to intrude on the strict appraisal of one's performance.

Oh, there were distractions all right at the launch site. A festival atmosphere prevailed. Colorful fiberglass boats sat on trailers and on car tops, rowers in bright uniforms spread out on the grass and spilled into the street, coaches and kids rode bicycles, officials and vendors and spectators spread out tents and barbecues and lawn chairs. An upstate New York town became a medieval fair for the day. But I had been to regattas before, and I paid the distractions little attention. I could think of little else but the race ahead.

At a regatta, a competitor spends very little time racing. I, for instance, arrived in town at 8:00 A.M. but my event was not scheduled to begin until 11:15 A.M. I devoted some of the intervening hours to chores, such as helping unload and rerig boats, and placing a card with the number my boat had been assigned—the number nine—in a slot at the bow. The main thing, I did, however, was wait: I talked, I stretched, I paced, I yawned, I cheered on teammates as they launched their boats. I got into a heated discussion with another masters sculler over the relative merits of aspirin, acetaminophen, and ibuprofen. Not that the masters rowers were a geriatric group. Of the nine competitors in the men's masters single event, some looked like former Olympians; others, ex-hippies. Some did not appear to be a day over the minimum masters age, twenty-seven; others had gray beards. At forty, I seemed to be in the middle.

Our race, like all the events, would begin with what amounted to an extended warm-up. At more or less the scheduled time, an official would announce the launching time for an event. Each competitor would then bring his boat to the dock and row westward along the river to the starting line, where he would turn around and race back toward the launching dock, just before which he would cross the finish line. He would row up hugging the north side and race down along the south side. Staying in lane was important, as races were scheduled all morning long; a wandering boat risked a collision with another, possibly bigger boat coming at top speed from the opposite direction.

Finally, an official called my race. "Men's masters single sculls," said a voice over a loudspeaker. I did not hurry down to the dock, for I was waiting for our club's entrant in the women's single sculls to return. We were sharing a boat. Once I saw her, I carried my oars onto the plastic dock. She had used a pair of hatchet-blade oars, while I preferred the old-fashioned goblet-shaped blade variety. I stood alongside the edge of the dock as she pulled in. I helped steady the boat as she got out.

"How did you do?" I asked.

"I don't know," she said. "I think I beat her." There had been only two competitors in her race.

"Terrific," I said, wondering if I would beat anyone in my race.

We quickly traded oars and then places. She stood on the dock, I got into the boat. I adjusted my bum in the wooden seat and got ready to push off from the dock.

"Hey," she called out, "do you have any trail mix?" She was standing on the dock beside our club's manager.

"Yes," I said, "in my van." My van? I hadn't driven to the race in a van; I didn't own a van. I meant to say "in my bag," that is to say, the gym bag I had brought with me and left beside the club's van.

"Are you nervous?" she asked.

"Who, me?" I said.

"You?" the manager said. "Ol' 'Flip' Strauss? Nervous?"

As I pushed off from the dock, stopped to tie my shoes, and then took my first strokes, I all but groaned at the recognition of how rusty I was. I felt sorely just how long it had been since my last scull. I felt acutely, moreover, just how tired I was. As I took the first turn, passed the finish line, and rowed under first one then a second bridge—one concrete, the other an elegant iron-and-steel trestle—my mood improved. I certainly was not going to achieve any personal best this day, but I had it in me, I knew, to finish the race after all. My strokes were long, my steering was straight, my back was erect, my eyes were focused. Although the riverbank meandered, the smoothness of the water made it easy to navigate. I realized something about the dreaded state of being alone in a scull: I enjoyed it. I relished the responsibility. I savored the freedom.

About a half-mile from the launching site, I began to relax enough to notice the surroundings. The riverside was quiet and parklike. Every now and then a house or dock broke the density of the trees, and once the road peeked through. I passed a heron whose posture mirrored my mood. Rather than striding confidently along the shore, he was sitting on a branch, body compressed, wings folded, shoulders drawn up to his head, gaze fixed ominously downward. He looked patriarchal, disapproving. What a portent! I laughed. If the signs were unfavorable, there was nothing to do but row hard and enjoy the race.

Admirably sane, but sobriety could not have prepared me for what happened next. Having rowed about a mile, I saw an island appear in the river ahead. I had a choice: I could keep to a steady course and row straight ahead, south of the island, or I could row around the north side of the island. The latter was a longer route, but with boats racing toward me on the south side of the river, it also seemed like a safer route.

I called out to the single astern of me, boat number three.

"Do we row on the north or south side of the island?" I shouted.

"I don't know," he called back.

On an impulse I headed north, around the island.

Number Three followed me, but in this case two heads were no better than one.

With clumps of weeds everywhere, the shallow channel north of the island was a mess. If I weaved my way carefully, however, I thought I could just make it through. Number Three maneuvered successfully, but I got stuck. With the end of the island in sight, my boat suddenly refused to go farther. I looked down at my oars and what I saw was this: green weeds wrapped around the oars like spinach pasta around a fork. I'll be damned, I thought. Stuck. Moving the blades was barely possible: it felt like rowing through mud. I had never heard of or even imagined any rowing experience like this, and was unsure just what to do. My port oar was freer than my starboard oar, so I tried backing the boat on the port side, in order to inch my way out again into clear water. I moved slowly and carefully, trying at all costs to avoid tipping the unstable shell. By now, seeing my distress, Number Three had stopped. It was a generous act; a more competitive sculler might have kept on going, seeing as I was in more bother than danger. He rowed over closer—though not too close—asked questions and called out encouragement.

"Keep trying," he said, "you'll get out." But I didn't. Progress was sluggish, at best; I figured the race would be long over by the time I got clear. Eventually we decided that Number Three should continue rowing toward the starting line and send help; there were likely to be motor boats along the course.

Left alone in the weeds, I mulled over my predicament. I was angry, no, furious; I was embarrassed, no, humiliated. I think I whimpered or moaned. I know that I called out, very loud, every four-letter word and then some. Of one more thing I am certain: I laughed. Heartily. Why not? Why not laugh at the extraordinary coincidence—the planets and stars must have been lined up—that had sent me to the adult equivalent of the Little League batter's box? There was no crowd to see me strike out, but my superego was delivering a whole stadiumfull worth of razzing.

In due time a police boat came. A diver got out, waded through the armpit-high water, and pulled the boat out into the clear. Finally: it had been a good twenty minutes since I had first got caught. It would be hard to forget the sensation when the diver pulled the last of the weeds off my starboard oar, a sensation like what I imagine the loosening of manacles to feel. Free at last! My oars felt as light as bamboo. I sculled briskly, trying to make up for lost time en route to the starting line.

"No excuses, no excuses, no excuses!" The refrain kept going through my mind as I rowed toward the starting line, passed by single scullers racing back along the south side of the river. But, damn it, it wasn't supposed to have been like this. I would shoulder the blame for having lost sleep before the race, I would take the rap for having decided to race in spite of my injuries and lack of practice, I would even allow that I might have been a little more cautious about the weeds. But was I to blame if my progress toward the starting line had been interrupted by what amounted to a twenty-minute session of weight lifting? Was I at fault if those cursed weeds had clutched the concentration out of me the way an octopus' tendrils hug the breath out of some fish? Well, in fact, I could have looked more closely at the map, posted by the race's organizers, on which the proper course was marked out, but I suppose that I was too anxious about my body that day to pay sufficient attention to the brain.

After rounding quite a few bends in the river I reached a straightaway. Ahead I could see a new concrete bridge and—farther in the distance than I would have liked—the starting line at last. I adjusted my form and did what I could to pull smartly over this last piece. As I approached the bridge, my friend Number Three emerged from under it, racing by in the other direction. To my surprise, he spoke.

"Have a good race, Nine!" he called out as he pulled by. Scullers are not supposed to waste energy on unnecessary conversation, but they are not supposed to work out with weeds either. Once again, Number Three showed what a gent he was.

I would like to have been a gent too: to have tipped my hat, bowed gravely, given my seat up to someone. All I could think of, though, was the basics: survival. I had finally reached the starting line, which was not actually a line, but rather two parallel lines of red buoys arranged to form a lane about fifty yards long by about ten yards wide. It looked like a section of an airport landing strip; they call it a chute. Race officials stood on a wooden dock along the shore.

"What's your event?" the head official called out.

"Men's masters singles," I called back.

"We've done quite a few of those," he said, with generous understatement. He told me to row past the chute, turn, and row into the chute at half pressure. As I expected, there would be no time to rest before the race began. So I turned the boat, took a deep breath, and rowed into the chute.

The character of a race depends entirely on your perspective. Looking down from a bridge, you fix your eyes on a passing shell as you would on a passing missile. You see the velocity, the efficiency, the accuracy. Thoughts of angles and calibrations occur to you; your mind speaks the language of trigonometry or photography. The crews look machinelike, while the rowers might be artworks of Socialist realism, muscles trained upon the common effort.

Looking ahead in the boat, however—and a good rower doesn't look up at the spectators on the bridge, no matter how loud they cheer—the race is only sweat and pain and panting and willpower. The race is not Socialist realism but abstract expressionism: it is a Kandinsky canvas, an attempt to impose order on separate blotches of form and color. Whether rowing in a single scull or an eight-oared crew, you are no machine but just someone working to keep his form straight and his concentration sure.

I've been in races where the paint somehow manages to get onto the canvas in the right configuration. I've been in races in a coxed four or eight in which the rower, freed of having to steer, has merely to do the impossible and not the unimaginable. Races that go like this: what with thinking about following stroke and keeping the catches and finishes clean and going slow on the slide during the recovery and trying not to think about the pain in every inch of the legs—even with all that going on, you somehow remember to breathe every now and then. Then you discover, to your amazement, that your boat is boat lengths ahead of the competition. They are riding your wake in defeat, and as you pull farther ahead you would daydream, if you could allow yourself to daydream, about reaching a slack and panting state of collapse in the bliss zone on the other end of the finish line.

I've also been in races where you can hardly get the paint out of the tube, like the summer my friends and I took a coxed four out against a boat of college rowers on their vacation: even had we been in peak condition they still would have had us beat within five strokes of the start. Then there was the first time I sat bow in a double scull race. It was the end of October, and given our difficulty keeping on a straight line, we were lucky that the worst that happened was the indignity of being passed right and left by kids in Halloween costumes. I've made false starts and missed strokes; I've lost the stroke's rhythm and I've caught a crab (that is, got the blade stuck in the water). Never before, though, had I raced in a shell that all but had the graffito IRONY smeared on the bow.

The row to the starting line had been an obstacle course; the row back to the finish was more like a Sunday stroll than a race. For about the first mile of the race I rowed alone. The loneliness was beautiful, but it was not a race. There was no jockeying for position, no passing other boats, no wakes to mind.

There were no other rowers. A solitary practice can be a killer workout, nonetheless, but not this one. I had rowed too fast from the weeds to the starting line, thereby using up energy I should have husbanded for the race. I knew this from the start, and even before, from the minute I reached midchute and the official told me I could begin rowing at full pressure. "Do I have to?" I felt like calling back. Instead I put my best effort into producing strong, hard strokes, or what would have been strong, hard strokes had I not been so rickety by then.

"From this point on the race is all yours." So the head official called as I left the chute behind. Were these, I wondered, words of puzzled encouragement, a polite suggestion that I start racing in earnest? Were they a veiled reminder that most of the other boats had long since finished? Or did he say this to every boat?

I started rowing harder and the wind picked up; I was rowing into a headwind. Great, I thought, that's all that was missing. The wind died as quickly as it had started though. The official was right, the race was all mine.

I rallied and pulled hard, then weakened, then rallied again. I rowed like a a surfer, riding waves: a wave of exertion, a wave of pain, a wave of exhaustion, a wave of stress, a wave of exhilaration.

What went wrong during the race? What didn't? My body felt pain, numbness and throbbing and flaming tendinitis. My form fell apart. It was as if everything that I had built up during the season fell down. It didn't fall with a crash; it wasn't the fall of an earthquake or an explosion. It fell gently, like the petals of a dying flower. I was aware of it, and frustrated by it, and yet somehow entertained by it, somehow able to watch it as if from a distance. I knew that I was going slowly—heck, I had faster Sunday strolls—but I also knew that I was out of gas. Every now and then I would take a deep breath, count to three, and start over, trying to get things right. But my arms had no strength, and my concentration was slack. Try as I might, I seemed unable to hold the proper form for more than about thirty seconds at a time.

I had lost my rhythm: instead of alternating a hard drive with a gentle recovery, I was pulling perfunctory strokes and racing through the recovery, neglecting to breathe, neglecting to recover. By failing to extend my body fully at the catch, I shortened up my stroke and deprived the boat of power. It was like swimming the breaststroke without the kick or the glide. I was moving the boat jerkily and inefficiently and without authority.

But I was moving the boat. Steering required considerable attention, which was a good thing, as it left me little time to think about my performance. The river's turns came up as quickly as those of a race course on some arcade game. There were buoys and metal posts to avoid and, having rowed in solitude for about a mile, there were now other boats. They passed in the opposite direction on the other side of the river, heading for the starting line for their races: elite (that is, under age twenty-seven) single scullers, high school eights. A quad from my boat club cheered as they passed me: "Go, Cascadilla!" Two girls stood on a dock and waved as I went by. I began to feel like a competitor again.

Now I heard shouting in the distance. Growing louder as I approached, it must, I decided, be the noise of spectators cheering. It was not. What I had heard turned out to be the sounds of kids playing basketball in a fenced-in court along the river. The ballplayers were calling passes and intent on the basket; they did not give the boats a glance.

I was on my own as I headed for a bridge, about 200 yards or so from the finish line, as I remembered from the start of my row—so long ago, as it seemed. I pulled out whatever energy I had left. Sitting erect, looking straight astern, I aimed for long and hard and perfect strokes. Out of breath and in pain, I drew satisfaction out of every creak of my ankles and every straining of my wrists. Every awkward motion up and down the slide, every determined pop of the blades from the water at the finish and every will-driven rising up on the stretchers at the catch gladdened me. Giddy and driven, I felt on each recovery as if I were gulping down champagne laced with caffeine. One more stroke and one more and one more and then I heard the horn. I had crossed the line and finished the race.

I was beat. I was beaten, and by a country mile. But I was beaming. As I sculled back easily to the dock, I glowed. There would be no one on the shore to slap my back and say "well done." There would be no brass band, no fireworks, no twenty-one-gun salute. There would, however, be one rower who gloried in the knowledge that he had acquired very exclusive bragging rights in a contest with himself. By rowing through the pain, by rowing the race at all, a certain Little League dropout knew that he had rounded the bases.

6

The Return

Ithaca has given you a good journey;
Without it you wouldn't have set out.
It has nothing more to give.

But if you find it poor, Ithaca didn't cheat you.
As wise as you've become, with such experience,
You'll understand what these Ithacas mean.

—C. P. CAVAFY, *Ithaca* (My translation)

The afterglow of that row back from the finish line disappeared quickly. First came my pride's fall. I should have known better, but I took it on the chin even so when I went to check my race time, posted on a wall at the race headquarters. It was no better than what I had done in a mediocre practice, and far slower than the next-slowest boat in my event.

Then came the morning after, on which my body declared rebellion. All my muscles were sore, and my right side sagged. I had a muscle spasm in my right shoulder and a cramp in my right calf. My right hand and foot felt numb. A visit to the chiropractor, a consultation with my physician, and reality stared me in the face. There would be no more sculling until I healed. Since the season had only a few weeks more to run, that effectively meant no more sculling until spring.

My troubles seemed to focus on the lower back, possibly a slipped disk, although that ailment is as tricky to diagnose as it is common. The lower back is a war zone among experts who are at odds over both cause and cure. For my part, I come to attribute my various aches and pains to multiple causes. The pain in my forearms, as I would learn in time, was tendinitis. It stems directly from a mistake in sculling technique: a big and basic mistake but one that, once recognized, is easily cured. The lower back pain owes something to poor posture which, whether inborn or bred of bad habit, predates my rowing. The back problems also owe something to my training techniques, especially running stadium stairs and skipping rope, because they may have led to overcompression of the spinal vertebrae. Perhaps the main culprit is not sports at all, but simply the stress and strain of middle-age life. Sitting at a desk, doing chores in the yard, carrying a lively twenty-five-pound one-year-old in a backpack—all these may have taken their toll on my back.

Yet sculling was out, for the time being. Swimming, on the other hand, might do some good. The sport offers a full-body workout and intense aerobic activity. It puts no strain on the back, and is indeed virtually injury free. I had never been more than an indifferent swimmer, however. To get the most out of the sport, I would need help.

I signed up for a masters swim class. When I met the coach, I found a bluff and friendly man of about thirty. He was looking for potential masters champions. I was looking for a level of minimal competence, enough to give me a good workout. We sized each other up, noted each other's stubbornness, and reached a meeting of minds. I would work my tail off. In exchange, he would teach me to clean off the accretion of bad habits that, over the years, had slowed my crawl to, well, ... I learn, for example, the difference between kicking properly, with ankles fully flexed and toes pointing behind me, and kicking as I had been, with ankles tensed and toes pointing downward. It is liberating to get the kick right. I learn to lead with the elbows on the recovery and to pull more efficiently on the drive. Now my swimming takes off, just as my oars flew on race day when they finally got free of the weeds.

Swimming is a fine sport. Like rowing, it is a water sport, and so the principles of fluid mechanics apply alike. Both swimmer and sculler use the arms or an extension of the arms (the oars) to anchor a fixed object (the body or the boat) which they each then drive forward. Both swimmer and sculler alternate drive and recovery, rhythmic breathing and exhalation. The catch—the moment when the hand or blade slices into the water and grabs hold of it—is crucial in both sports. Both swimmer and sculler have to master difficult and by no means intuitive techniques. If shell and oars add a mechanical complexity to rowing which is absent in swimming, the reliance of the swimmer on the body and little else intensifies the demands on endurance. In other words, the rower, especially the single sculler, pays a heavier price than the swimmer for slackening concentration on technique, but five miles of swimming the freestyle takes more out of a body than does five miles in a single scull.

Although sculling offers a superb workout, minute for minute, swimming offers a better one. The equipment—a bathing suit, the membership fee for joining a pool—is cheaper for swimmers than for scullers. While daylight and wind and rain and fog and winter limit a sculler's time on the water, an indoor pool operates on a regular schedule year-round. Then there is the difference in preparation time. By the time a sculler brings oars and boat down to the dock and is ready to row, the swimmer will be well into a workout. In addition to these practical advantages, swimming may even offer a royal road to inner peace. With so few distractions in the water, the swimmer finds it easier than the sculler to relax. After only a few lessons, the swimmer is able to think of finding a quiet spot inside, a firm place, as it were, on which to build fine technique. Such grace descends less easily on the sculler.

I am glad that my injuries forced me to take a swim class. I feel lucky to be able to add so practical a sport to my athletic repertory. Swimming will make an excellent substitute for stadium running and skipping rope. What it will not do, however, is replace rowing. I am eager to get back into a single scull as soon as I can. But can that be?

Would I indeed do it all again, even knowing about the injuries, even knowing that my first race in a single would send my pride up the river?

Two years went by before I got back in a boat. It took months for my injury to heal. Once it had, the chiropractor gave me a clean bill of health. He said there was no medical reason not to row again. Yet I was in no rush to risk reinflammation. Between a new assignment at work and the growth of my kids, moreover, time was at a premium; what I had of it for fitness I decided to give to swimming. After a weekend at a masters swimming clinic my technique had taken off, and I was doing laps eagerly. Finally, there was my ego. Rowing again meant running the risk of being pointed at as the kid who got stuck in the weeds. No thanks.

Yet one day toward the end of the second summer since my debacle, I headed down to the boathouse without thinking or wavering and renewed my membership. Here's my check, thanks for the key, see you on the water: presto. I'd like to say that a day of enchanting beauty or transfiguring heat or suffusing light after a storm had inspired me but, in fact, it was an ordinary summer afternoon. What, then, made me go back?

Rowing exists at the edge of pain, the edge of heartbreak, the edge of epiphany. It inspires nostalgia and

devotion. Three anecdotes might help explain my decision that day.

The first anecdote comes from a weekend I spent at a
sculling clinic in southern Ontario. Among the other students were three women from Sudbury. It is a mining
town, I remembered, thinking back to junior high geography class, short on charm and long on nickel—and winter.
Chatting with one of the women confirmed my memory.
She told me that they were three of the four rowers of a
coxed four. They rowed on a northern lake. Their club has
no boathouse and no dock, so the rowers had to carry the
boat into the chilly water themselves. The water is so cold
that they had to wear wetsuits when the season opens in
late May, and they had to stop rowing in late September. A
dock would keep them out of the water and add an extra
month to the season, two weeks at either end, but the club
has no money for such luxuries.

Yet the women rowed, without complaining. They
were forty-year-olds, like me, and the only time they could
all fit into their busy schedules was five-thirty in the morning, so that is when they rowed. It wasn't habit that made
them do it, because they were all midlife rowers; they had
no memories of college days to buoy them. Nor was it
comfort, because rowing, as it turned out, sent them each
regularly to the chiropractor. They rowed because they
loved the camaraderie and the dedication and the water.

The second anecdote comes from Manhattan. I sat at
the bar of a private club off Fifth Avenue one day drink-

ing hard liquor with an old friend. At three in the afternoon on a weekday alcohol is decadent but we didn't give
a damn. Another friend of ours was in the hospital and we
needed to drink to him. We talked about old times and
philosophized in our cups when suddenly my friend
started to fly solo. He is a lot older than I and of a generation with a roomy tolerance for nostalgia. I braced myself
for a weepy rehash of his first love or of the Korean War.
To my amazement, though, what followed was a perfect
rendition of his college crew song.

I was too surprised to take notes but I wish I had. The
music sounded like every other college fight song I've ever
heard but I liked the nineteenth-century feel of the lyrics.
I am sure that the last words were the admonition,
"Stroke! Stroke! Stroke!" Also, if I'm not mistaken, this
memorable couplet turned up somewhere in the middle:

> The wild delight of knowing
> `Tis our power that does the rowing!

I phoned my friend afterward to get the words but,
sobered up, he denied all knowledge of them.

What is it about rowing that made it and not memories
of the backseat or the perfect wave into the equivalent of
a swan dive off a cliff into the waters of remembrance?
The remembered rhythm of the stroke? The comfort of
group feeling? The memory of youthful prowess? The
soothing quality of water? I wish I knew. If I did I could
set up my shingle and make it as a therapist.

Maybe the third anecdote explains rowing's appeal. It too comes from the weekend clinic in Ontario. We rowed there on Martindale Pond, just south of Lake Ontario. It is a beautiful and stirring site. The shores are hilly and lined with willows and maples, an occasional boulder affording a hint of glacial terrain and of the Canadian shield farther north. Here, every July, they hold the Royal Canadian Henley Regatta, a hundred-year-old race. We could see the grandstand and we even rowed across the starting line.

All of this is prologue to the story, a vignette from a solo row I took. It was a Saturday evening at the end of August, around six o'clock. It was still light out but a full moon had risen. Both wind and water were calm. Alone, I enjoyed the still, exquisite scene. Suddenly another boat came into view. As it drew closer I made out a single rowed by an experienced-looking guy about my age. He must have sized me up as a visiting novice enrolled in the clinic.

"One night like this and you're hooked for life," he called out knowingly.

I have no idea why I went back to rowing that day and every idea.

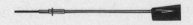

My senses are extra-sharp in this second incarnation as a rower. I came back for the tail end of the summer and for the fall. Every color, every breeze, every smell of those seasons registered.

I rowed the old five-mile course on the inlet. At the narrows the water was just as I had remembered—smooth, glossy, soft, yielding—but the landscape had changed. A huge construction project was in full swing. They had almost finished building a new, second bridge right next to the old bridge, just a few yards to its north, and about fifty yards farther north they had poured into place the concrete pylon for the third. Alone and unspanned, shiny white in the dark green water against a grassy background of parkland, the pylon looked like a monolith, the boundary stone of another world. The new bridge was so close to and so well aligned with the old bridge that, from a distance, they didn't seem like separate spans. As the boat neared, the sound of workmen hammering and banging on roadbed rang out. Water droplets, left over from violent thunderstorms of the night before, poured off the sides of the steel span, like some tropical waterfall. I rowed through warily.

The autumn days made the deepest impression this year. At 6:30 A.M. in October it's still dark out. So we row with a flashing strobe light attached to the bow of each boat. It's eery and secretive to row in the dark, as if we are part of some predawn naval raid. There's nothing like being on the water to watch the first rays of daylight. Yet other times of the day can charm as well.

One Tuesday, for example, I bolted from the office just before noon and went for a row. Twelve is an odd hour to be on the water in the inlet, as the north wind often blows then. On the fifteenth of October though, in upstate New

York, a bright, sunny day is precious, even a day on which the temperature only reaches fifty degrees Fahrenheit; soon the high would be only fifteen. So I dropped everything and headed for the boathouse. There was indeed a chop on the water as I set out, but only a slight one. The wind was out of the north but it was barely a breeze, only an exhalation to scatter the clouds. All that was left was light and color.

The sky was as blue as a marathoner's veins after a race. The water ran navy, dark and reflective like tinted glass. Between sky and lake, on hills stretching into the distance, stood files of trees with autumn leaves. The flaming trees on a ridge to the stern look like apples on one big, greened-leafed tree. Is there a language with a hundred and fifty words for red? You would need them all in order to describe the range of colors, from orange to flame to gold to scarlet to crimson, turning the hills into hosannas, hushed but ecstatic.

However gorgeous the scenery, beauty was not the keynote of my short season of rowing that year; diligence was.

It was a time to remember the good and repudiate the bad, to sing an old song with a new faith. I wanted to row hard but I wanted to row smart. The season, however little remained of it, would prove decisive. In retrospect, the time off had served me well. Swimming had made me looser and more flexible, as I noticed the first time I stepped back in a boat. I sat up spontaneously taller, as if I had grown several inches. Swimming also paid off pedagogically. I spent much of my time in the pool practicing drills, taught at the swim clinic, that fostered learning through the body as much as the mind. They worked, both in the water and on it, to judge by the ease with which I now picked up new tricks of the trade.

It took no time at all for me to feel comfortable again in a boat. I moved quickly from training tub back to racing single. I was out of shape but in form, that is, my technique snapped back nearly to where it had been when I last sculled two years before. Yet my mind-set had shifted. Swimming had stamped an impress of style on me, attuning my body to every lapse and infelicity. It was one thing to scull happily along, another to do so with grace and efficiency. I was making mistakes, familiar errors, like slouching and bending at the waist rather than the hips, and faults that I didn't know existed much less that I was guilty of, such as not smiling—smiling at the catch being a terrific way to stay relaxed, as I learned. Such knowledge comes from coaching, which is what I needed.

Between the help of a former college rower at the boat club who went out with me several times in a double and a weekend sculling clinic out of town, I managed to change my habits. My partner in the double told me that he could feel me rowing with the arms rather than the legs and back. The result was deadly. By neglecting the body's strongest muscles I was generating too little power. Furthermore, by favoring the upper body, I tended to hold the handles of the oars too high, which meant in turn that the blades went too low, that is, too deep into the water, turning them into twin anchors: my old nemesis. To "lift the anchors" and to move the boat with power I would need to change the balance of the body. That would take concentration. The instructors at the clinic made subtler observations still. They pointed out, to my surprise, that on the recovery my left hand was above the right rather than in front of it. A videotape showed the error clearly, as it did the general tension of my posture in the boat. The most important lesson of the clinic, however, and one that spoke directly to the tendinitis of my maiden race in a single scull, concerned my wrists.

At the finish the sculler must pop the oars out of the water. My habit, as I learned, was to get the oars up by bending or dropping my wrists. The proper technique, however, is to leave the wrists relatively flat and to drop the elbows. Yet that technique requires in turn that the sculler hold the oar handle correctly, and it turned out that I wasn't doing that right either. The sculler needs to get the fingers wound far enough around the handle so that the palm is flat and the top knuckles are bent. He needs, furthermore, to position the thumb on the end of the handle so that he can move the oar from square to feather and back by using the fingers more than the wrist. The maneuver sounds more complicated than it is. Stretch the hands, practice the motion, and soon it becomes smooth and natural. A week later it seems astonishing to have ever tried to feather the oars any other way.

It felt like a different body in the boat that autumn; it felt like a different sport. I made the recovery slow and the drive strong and sharp. I moved my arms quickly at the finish, followed with the back, and then came up the slide with my legs until, finally, at the catch, I pushed off the footstretcher with the feet. The boat went farther and faster and the sculler conserved energy. Then there was the biggest change of all, working with the legs and back more than the arms. I added power to the stroke and got the blades off the water, which took drag off the boat.

On an autumn morning I rowed more fluidly than I ever thought I had in me, and I rowed faster. It felt more like dancing than working out. I never thought I could sit up so strong and tall. I was discovering new muscles in my lower back, muscles on either side of the spine that hold it up.

With the blades consistently off the water the boat took off suddenly, as if crossing the street turned in an instant into breaking the sound barrier. I was flying now and wondering whether I wasn't afraid of flying. Too late now, too late for refastening the training wheels, but there was a small question about the engine. My heart could not keep up with the abrupt leap into speed. To have a shot at a race I would have to spend the winter training my aerobic capacity—as well as building strength and practicing form. But did I want to have a shot at a race?

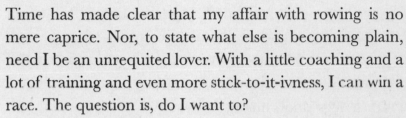

Time has made clear that my affair with rowing is no mere caprice. Nor, to state what else is becoming plain, need I be an unrequited lover. With a little coaching and a lot of training and even more stick-to-it-ivness, I can win a race. The question is, do I want to?

I realize that I have never taken seriously the possibility that I could succeed. I expect to lose; losing becomes me. I exist in a comfortable stasis of failure. But I could win at rowing if I worked as hard in the gym at building up strength and endurance as I've been working in the boat at improving my body form and blade technique. Rowing is about breaking through barriers. It trains the body to teach the mind how much farther and faster it can go than it had thought. To win requires concentration, dedication, and a retreat from irony.

To win requires believing in yourself. It's much easier to say, "Nah, never could do it" and to be able to slack off in the shadows than to have to work your backside off and to lay it on the line in an arena where losing would hurt your feelings; in an arena where you want to win and you want it badly. "No follow through"; "You can take a horse to water but you can't make him drink." Same old problems as in the Little League. But I'm smarter and battle-scarred and cunning now, and I know enough to correct my course and to get it right. I'd like to think of myself as a winner.

Learning to row at forty is a test. It's an audit of achievement and disappointment, both of which there has been plenty of since leaving college. It's about a second chance at something simple and verifiable. It's about reconcentrating and refocusing. So much of my career seems to me, in retrospect, to have been a process of retreat, hiding, avoidance of the big tests, caused in equal parts by diffidence, fear of failure, and laziness.

What I cherish about rowing is its simplicity. It's a controlled experiment. Never mind everything else: can you pass this test? Can you concentrate? Can you focus? Sculling is relatively simple. Either you are fit, technically masterful, concentrated, self-confident, and relaxed—or you're not. Neither office politics nor mating and raising a family nor the need to make money plays a major role. It's just you and the boat.

I make my decision.

This year, I resolved, I would do it right. As soon as we closed up the boathouse for the season in November, I began a systematic program of winter training. It would be a regular grind of exercise—six days a week—to build endurance, strength, speed, and flexibility. I wanted to up my potential both to go the distance and to generate short bursts of energy. I also wanted to hone my form and, especially important in my case, my posture. Nutrition, I was confident, could take care of itself, mainly because my wife took care of me. I don't eat junk food nor many desserts. My diet is full of fruits and vegetables and pasta and protein and I make sure to get some fat too. So I could focus on workouts.

I boned up on sports texts and jawboned with other, more knowledgeable rowers. Together, we put together a menu of weight lifting, stretching, swimming, stair climbing, stationary bicycle riding and, most important, ergometer rowing. The latter became to my training program what a pommel horse was to a medieval knight.

The Concept II rowing ergometer is manufactured by a company in Vermont run by former U.S. Olympians in rowing. It is a simple piece of equipment in metal, plastic, and wood. The designers used a flywheel and a slide to make a fair approximation of what it feels like to row on the water. The Concept II ergometer is a successful concept indeed, one that is now in its third phase—model A of the seventies having given way to model B of the eighties and now model C of the nineties. It has become a standard part of the rower's training tool kit.

Ergometer is Greek for "work meter." The meter in question is a performance monitor: a computer in a small box, attached to the top of the flywheel cage and facing the rower as she comes up the slide. The monitor counts revolutions of the wheel and measures distance (in meters), energy expended (in calories), and hypothetical effort (in watts). It can be set to count down various times or distances, for example, forty minutes or 5,000 meters. A common measure is the so-called 500-meter split, that is, the amount of time it takes to row 500 meters. If rowing is a trial then the ergometer is the courtroom, the meter is the jury. And an honest jury at that, because the numbers do not lie.

I come to love the numbers and to hate them. I teach myself to look straight ahead so that I'm not staring down at the display, but I soon discover that on the newest model ergometer the display can be adjusted upward into your line of sight. No escape. You can program workouts of short intervals or long distances into the meter, easy workouts or killers, aerobic or anaerobic workouts. You can purchase a pulse meter and measure your heart rate. My eyes glaze over when I dip too deeply into the terminology of high-tech exercise, but I admire those who master it, so I try at least to vary my workouts over the course of the week. One day is long distance, a second day is for intervals, a third day is for anaerobic threshold (that is, short bursts of energy). Two days are for weights—preceded, to be sure, by brief stints on the ergometer, and a sixth day is for swimming. On the seventh day I rest.

Rowers usually refer to the machine, affectionately or resignedly, as the erg. A monosyllable preceded by the article, as in the rack or the whip. It is as tough a machine as it is simple. It is commonly found in health clubs and commonly left unused, sleek but forlorn. Small wonder: think of aerobics plus weight lifting minus the music or camaraderie. Combine unalloyed endurance with straightforward strength and demand poise, timing, and practiced form as well. Think of pure pain: that's the ergometer.

Those who use the erg regularly may do so with devotion. They have a newsletter and world rankings and races, especially in the winter, in the United States climaxing in the mid-February CRASH-B race in Cambridge, Massachusetts. The acronym stands for "Charles River All-Star Has-Beens" or "Charles River Association of Sculling Has-Beens." The course in these races is 2,000 meters, about a mile and a quarter: that is, the performance monitor is set to count down to zero from that distance. The top ergometer racers can cover 2,000 meters in under six minutes; a beginner could do it in eight minutes. My efforts fall in the seven-minutes-plus range. The number calls to mind the game we used to play as preadolescents, Seven Minutes in Heaven, the difference being that a stint on the erg is distinctly purgatorial if not infernal.

Boats are about water, its grace and equivocation. The ergometer, by contrast, is landlocked; compared to a single scull it works in only two dimensions instead of three. Yet some rowers never get on the water at all, never feel the wind; they race only on the ergometer. What they lose in scenery and inspiration they gain in convenience and in power. The erg has fewer inertia problems than a scull on the water because the erg is fixed and motionless while a scull is always moving. So, all other things being equal, the erg is easier to power than is a scull.

The erg may breed the illusion that you can muscle your way through a medium that demands subtlety, that is no more susceptible to manhandling than is mercury. If so, the erg has been misused; those who know it well understand that it cannot, any more than a racing shell, be mastered by mindless muscle. That the erg too requires technique and agility should teach even the burliest rower that, come spring, the water will yield most easily to those who balance power with finesse.

I think about this as the training season begins in November. One must think about the erg because there is certainly no other distraction. Forget scenery, forget the inlet at daybreak. Here in the gym on the erg there is nothing to look at except the empty stationary bike opposite and the bulletin board behind it. On one side, the Nautilus machines stretch off into the distance, on the other side stand the NordicTracks. Behind and below is a racquetball court. In the gym you are a caveman, not an explorer; you sit tall, but psychologically you are huddled against the freezing cold rather than spread out with the breast open to the wind; you are drawn to lightbulbs and a boom box rather than to the lighthouse and the flapping of birds' wings, bound by noise and company rather than released by silence and solitude.

On the erg, unlike the water, you dare to think about stopping for a second to wipe off the sweat dripping down your nose, but your other psychic energy goes into revving up power and refining technique. Just sitting there, stationary, without moving an inch, and without bladework to think about or having to turn to see what's off the bow, well, then there's nothing else to do but power it. There's plenty of time to think about pushing with the legs which, believe me, I did. On a November day, about an hour after my workout, my thighs feel as if they've been through a pasta maker. There's plenty of time to think about making the stroke start from the feet, which worked so well that I might have dug holes in my sneakers. My back and my arms were merely levers, there only for the convenience of my legs. I think my lower back got stretched out an inch at either end in order to extend the connection between handle and footstretchers and thereby lengthen the stroke. Likewise the muscles around my armpit: they feel longer too.

The erg does a great job of building rhythm and consistency into the stroke. After staring at the flashing numbers long enough you begin to feel in your bones the difference between stroke rates of twenty-four and twenty-five. You develop perfect pitch for the difference in intensity on the footstretcher of say, quarter pressure and three-eighths pressure. The sensitivity is something to transfer to the water. Not so the stale, indoor atmosphere of a gym. Outside on the water, your sweat evaporates, but in the gym it seems there is nowhere for it to go except down your forehead to form puddles on your T-shirt.

The erg makes you feel like a collection of separate body parts: legs, back, arms. Even so small an object as the head carries weight, both literally and figuratively. The head needs to be upright or it will check the boat on the drive, adding too much weight to stern. Yet it is the large muscles that garner most of the rower's attention. Between concentrating on the leg drive and lifting weights and massaging sore muscles, a rower spends an awful lot of time thinking about his or her thighs. This strikes me as both arcane and hard-core. Vanity might drive a body to flatten the belly or build up "beach biceps," but the thigh is a strictly business kind of muscle. The rower is like a cowboy who instead of choosing the right hat or chaps or spurs, concentrates his attention on his saddle pad. What choice is there? To ride a bronco or power a scull, you've got to do what it takes. The thigh may be uncouth but it gets the job done, for a substantial part of the power of the stroke comes from the spring off the stretcher.

The erg, in short, teaches you to be efficient. The erg is all mechanics, all strength and conditioning and rhythm: all Rome, no Greece. Except, that is, for the inspired madness of the very enterprise, of subjecting your body to a kind of moving rack, which is pure Greek in its impracticality.

The erg is not without its mystery. Consider the way that you let yourself go and build up a head of steam, how you generate a crescendo of power and yet all the while remain in control: you can adjust the dial, as it were, and bring the rating up slightly from twenty-four to twenty-five strokes per minute, you can ratchet up the pressure on the footstretchers or ease off. You become like the ocean, roaring onto the shore in great rolling breakers and then waning silently, like the moon, only to come pounding back, as liberated from friction as the wind. On the water the sculler moves to an eighteenth-century beat or perhaps to jazz, but whether Mozart or Miles Davis, the music is light and understated. The erg, by contrast, is a nineteenth-century symphony, all the instruments blasting; it's big music, like Mahler or Tchaikovsky. Yet even so, you are the conductor; one flick of the baton and the music halts. The erg is about controlled frenzy.

By December my times are coming down dramatically. It's a big boost if also, as it turns out later, beginner's luck. By February the rate of improvement has slowed to a snail's pace. I prize every second then that I can shave off my time.

By December I also miss the inlet badly, but I am becoming adept at taking scenic beauty where I find it. At 6:15 on the darkest morning of the winter, just days before Christmas, I am in the car and pulling out of the driveway, heading for the gym. Yesterday afternoon and evening saw the first good-size snowfall of the year (it has been a dry season) and the ground is covered with several inches of fresh powder. Overnight the storm has blown by, and though it is still dark out, the stars, as bright as they are sparse at this hour, signal that it is going to be a sunny day.

Nearly two months of rowing on the erg shifts your center of gravity. My thighs feel stronger than they've ever been. When walking I feel as if my gait has shifted upward from my calves. When rowing, my stroke feels as if it's mainly legs: which is good, since that is just what the text-books say it is supposed to be. When I was on the water I needed constant reminders not to snatch, that is, not to start the stroke with the arms. The stroke, rather, has got to begin with the power of the legs. "Push before you pull" is the motto I needed to have engraved on my forehead:

that is, put pressure on the footstretchers with the heels before putting power into the arms.

Yet I must not overdo it. The back and arms, remember, have to begin moving at the same time as the legs, though with less intensity; otherwise you would shoot the slide. The need to make the drive a single motion with varying emphases rather than a collection of three separate motions—that continues to bear repeating.

So does the need to sit up straight at the finish and at the catch. Even on the erg I have to display constant vigilance, especially at the finish, where my back has a tendency to sag, which makes it harder to set up legs for the position of maximum power at the catch. When I do sit tall, when I do place the body parts just where I want them, then I'm really cooking on every stroke. I'm taut, I feel like an engine whose power radiates from the thighs.

I practice racing. Every Saturday I do a 2,000-meter dry run. My times improve steadily, but they could be even better, were they not bedeviled by those two old enemies, form and breathing. Upon feeling like reaching for an oxygen mask after my practice race on two consecutive Saturdays, I realize that my problem is simple: I have been holding my breath. I have to remember to breathe on every stroke: inhale on the recovery, exhale on the drive. I need to smile at the catch as a way of relaxing.

My form, never more than a work in progress, needs constant adjustment as well. I take my cue not only from the performance meter but from sensations as well, from sights, sounds, and feelings. For example, I traveled a lot that winter and so worked out in different gyms. Once in a tony health club I found myself rowing beside a wall-to-ceiling mirror. It was unnerving at first to see my every move and mistake reflected, but once I got used to it the mirror became a good check.

Sound helped too. When you are on the erg your mind is too busy to pay attention to the sounds of the machine; you notice only that they are indeed loud. When you are off the machine and hear someone else use it, then you discern the individual sounds of the different phases of the rowing stroke, but most of the time what you hear is wrong. Most people who use the erg don't know how to use it right. They don't attain full extension on the stroke, they pull with their arms when they should be pressing with their legs and, worst of all, they don't take their time recovering up the slide. Instead they go from stroke to stroke with virtually no rest at all, with the unsurprising result of quick exhaustion: few people at the gym seem to spend more than five or ten minutes on the erg. What you hear from such exercises is an all-but-continuous, discordant rattle: up the slide, down the slide, up the slide down.

Every so often you find an indoor rower who knows what she is doing on the erg, and then the sounds fall out in bright, marching order, a rhythm as precise and unmistakable as a marine drill squad showing off for a hometown crowd. The rower drives down the slide and transfers power to the flywheel, which in turn spins out a long, low, intensifying *whoosh* for one beat. Then, as the rushing sound subsides, there follow clicks and ratcheting for three beats as the rower slowly works back up the slide to the start of another stroke. *Whoosh, click, click, click . . . whoosh, click, click, click,* and on and on. I learned to cock an ear for those sounds in my own stroke.

Sound and sensation, form and breathing: perhaps the whole thing can be summed up as mental focus. Concentration is crucial. My mind wants to wander, but good rowing demands steady attention. Indeed, bodily strength and aerobic fitness will make a better rower but it is mental discipline that pays the greatest dividends. So I work on concentrating until I've honed my thoughts to a point so sharp that it could burn a hole through the underbrush of daydreams and anxieties. Sometimes I repeat a nonsensical jingle, "Form before function, form before function."

When you finally get the ergometer down right you can feel the stroke rising from the feet up through the legs to the torso, climbing up the back and down the arms, making a quick exit through the wrists across the hands and out the fingers. You can feel yourself suspended from the oar, as my first instructor promised so long ago. You can feel the length of your whole body, stretched out and supple, bent like a bow from the heels to the knuckles. You can feel yourself pivoting at the heels like a diver springing from the high board or a long jumper taking off from his mark or an artiste turning around and around the trapeze. Your body completes a circle from handle to flywheel to footstretcher, continuous, without beginning or end, smooth as a wheel.

You are uncertain where the machine begins and the body ends. You sense the danger of slipping into cliché about "oneness" or "wholeness" or Zen, but if the sandal fits, wear it. However far you may still be from the rower you would like to become, you find it hard to believe that you have come so far, that you are the same man as the gangly klutz who first sat slouching on a wooden boat seat.

A fine layer of snow still covers the ground in upstate New York, but here and there the green shoots are visibly poking through. The wind blows from a different direction. It is light out now at six in the morning and the sun goes down later each night.

A winter dedicated to the ergometer has given me a lot in return, from the rhythm of the stroke and the feel of the trained body, to the sense of hard-won poise and symmetry, of muscles and lungs pushed to the limit. Yet it is not enough.

I want the promise of water. I want the paradox of pain and passion, but if I did not have a taste for paradox I would never have got into a single scull in the first place. Power poised on fragility, an angel's feathers and a bull's back, poetry in calluses: these are the elements that first drew me to sculling and that draw me back again. I took up rowing less to win medals than to take risks. Every injury, every flip, every stroke squeezed out through the pain is a sign not of failure but of success. Every ounce of determination to do better than the poor race time weighs in favor of following your dreams.

I will follow them again soon. I yearn for the beauty of the inlet at dawn. I miss the smell of varnished wood in the boat bay. I miss the sight of the dock disappearing in the horizon. I miss the sound of blades slipping in and out of the water. I miss the touch of the long, long pull from bow to stern. I miss the ghost fleets of ancient Greek ships. I miss the herons. I miss the crisp mornings on the water in the October sunlight. I miss the nervous confirmation of racing.

The inlet is waiting.

Suggested Readings

What follows is a personal selection rather than a complete bibliography. Most of the books concern rowing but I have also included a few other works on subjects such as history and philosophy. Additional reading can be found cited in the books below; for excellent bibliographies on rowing history, see in particular the works by Dodd, Gardiner, Ivry, and Mendenhall. Other good sources of information on current rowing are *American Rowing*, the bimonthly magazine of the United States Rowing Association, and the biweekly *Independent Rowing News*.

Adams, Noah. *Piano Lessons.* New York: Delacorte Press, 1996. A journalist's witty, engaging, and sympathetic account of taking up the piano in midlife.

Amit, M. *Athens and the Sea. A Study in Athenian Sea Power.* Collection Latomus 74. Brussels: Latomus, 1965. A detailed, scholarly introduction to the classical Athenian navy (ca. 400 B.C.) and to its rowers.

Bourne, Gilbert C. *A Textbook on Oarsmanship.* Oxford: Oxford University Press, 1923. A well-established and comprehensive study, still in print, of rowing technique and the body, written by an anatomist.

Burnell, Richard. *The Complete Sculler.* Toronto: Sport Books Publisher, 1989 [1977]. Burnell, an Olympian and author of several books on rowing, here provides a concise and practical introduction to sculling technique.

Cartledge, P. A. "The Machismo of the Athenian Empire—or the Reign of the Phaulus." In L. Foxhall and J. Salmon, eds. *When Men Were Men: Masculinity, Power, and Identity in Classical Antiquity.* London: Routledge, 1998. A lively and scholarly discussion of the culture of rowers in classical Athens.

Casson, Lionel. *Ships and Seafaring in Ancient Times.* Austin: University of Texas Press, 1994. This well-written book offers an overview of the subject by a leading scholar of ancient maritime history.

Churbuck, D. C. *The Book of Rowing.* Woodstock, NY: The Overlook Press, 1988. A comprehensive introduction by a rower and journalist, covering history, lore, technique, workouts, and boat types. Illustrated with black-and-white photographs and line drawings.

Cooper, Helen A., ed. *Thomas Eakins—The Rowing Pictures.* With contributions by Martin A. Berger, Christina Currie, Amy R. Werbel. New Haven: Yale University Art Gallery, Yale University Press, 1996. This exhibition catalog contains good reproductions of paintings and drawings as well as insightful scholarly essays on Eakins's technique, career, and interest in rowing and on the symbolism of rowing in Victorian culture.

Cunningham, Frank and Leslie Stillwell Strom. *The Sculler at Ease. What Makes Boats Go.* Boulder, CO: Avery Press, 1992. A graceful book, offering a gentle yet pragmatic approach to sculling by an expert coach. It contains gems of insight plus stylish writing and poetic imagery. This little book merits reading and rereading.

Decker, Wolfgang. *Sports and Games of Ancient Egypt.* Translated by Alan Guttman. New Haven: Yale University Press, 1992. Includes a good discussion of rowing as well as photographs of Egyptian representations of rowing. The author, an Egyptologist, is an expert on ancient athletics.

Dodd, Christopher. *The Story of World Rowing.* London: Stanley Paul, 1992. A lively and thorough introduction to the history of rowing in war and peace from the Greeks to the present day.

Edwards, H.R.A. *The Way of a Man with a Blade.* London: Routledge and Kegan Paul, 1963. A memoir by an English rowing coach. They don't make them like this anymore.

Fairbairn, Ian, ed. *Steve Fairbairn on Rowing.* London: The Kingswood Press, 1990. A collection of writings by the great and iconoclastic early-twentieth-century Cambridge coach who emphasized bladework, balance, and natural body movements, whereas contemporary conventional wisdom demanded strict precision at every point in the stroke cycle. In his own way, Fairbairn was an unconscious Zen master; his prose is epigrammatic.

Ferriss, John A., ed. *Rowing Fundamentals: A Manual for Coaches.* Indianapolis: United States Rowing Association, 1981. A very useful collection of essays, articles, and diagrams by various coaches covering nearly every aspect of technique and training. The emphasis is on sweep rowing but there is much here for the sculler too.

Gardiner, Robert, ed. *The Age of the Galley. Mediterranean Oared Vessels Since Preclassical Times.* Conway's History of the Ship. Annapolis, MD: Naval Institute Press, 1995. A basic reference book by scholarly authorities covering the period from the third millennium B.C. to the Renaissance. The sixteen chapters range from general to technical subjects, including the trireme, and are well illustrated.

Grahame, Kenneth. *The Wind in the Willows*. New York: Grosset & Dunlop, 1966. This children's classic, originally published in 1908, is well worth an adult's while. Through the adventures of four animals who live along a river, the book gently caricatures scullers and hobby enthusiasts in general. It includes the memorable pronouncement that absolutely nothing is more fun than "simply messing about in boats."

Halberstam, David. *The Amateurs*. New York: William Morrow, 1985. The noted journalist traces four American elite male scullers on their way to competition at the 1984 Los Angeles Olympics. It makes an exciting story.

Hale, John R. "The Lost Technology of Ancient Greek Rowing." *Scientific American*. 27.5 (May 1996): 82–87. An archaeologist and rower argues, against most scholars, that the Athenian trireme employed not fixed-seat rowing but, rather, allowed rowers to slide back and forth upon cushions on their benches. A good piece of historical detective work.

Hilary, Richard. *The Last Enemy*. New York: St. Martin's, 1971. [1943]. A memoir of the Battle of Britain by an RAF fighter pilot (who died in action later in World War II), this book begins with an account of rowing among the *jeunesse dorée* of prewar Oxford. The author's tale of camaraderie between British and German oarsmen at international competitions before the war evokes an aristocratic sporting world that is no more.

Herrigel, Eugen. *Zen in the Art of Archery*. With an introduction by D. T. Suzuki. Translated by R.F.C. Hull. New York: Vintage Books, 1989. A German philosophy professor, teaching in Japan, masters the discipline of Buddhist archery and finds inner peace. Beautifully written.

Holt, John. *Never Too Late. My Musical Life Story*. A Merloyd Lawrence Book. New York: Delacorte Press/Seymour Lawrence, 1978. An educator takes up the cello in his forties, falls in love with it, and learns "that our lives and possibilities are not determined and fixed by what happened to us when we were little."

Ivry, Benjamin. *Regatta. A Celebration of Oarsmanship.* New York: Simon and Schuster, 1988. Witty, idiosyncratic, and substantive essays by a nonrower who emphasizes the aesthetic of the sport. Excellent color photographs.

Kelley, Robert F. *American Rowing. Its Background and Traditions.* New York: G. P. Putnam's Sons, 1932. A grand narrative in the old style, full of anecdotes. The author was rowing correspondent of the *New York Times,* in the days when newspapers like the *Times* had rowing correspondents.

Kiesling, Stephen. *The Shell Game. Reflections on Rowing and the Pursuit of Excellence.* New York: William Morrow, 1982. A Yale oarsman's classic essay on competition, teamwork, and the pursuit of self-mastery. Written with vigor and irony.

———. *The Complete Recreational Rower & Racer. From Indoor Rowing Machines to Outdoor Shells.* New York: Crown, 1990. A practical guide to recreational sculling written with verve by a noted oarsman and rowing author. Useful and crisp photos by Jinsey Dauk Kiesling.

Kyle, D. G. *Athletics in Ancient Athens.* Leiden: E. J. Brill, 1987. A good introduction to the subject, it offers only a brief discussion of rowing, as one might expect, since rowing was more naval activity than sport in ancient Greece.

Lambert, Craig. *Mind Over Water: Lessons on Life from the Art of Rowing.* Boston and New York: Houghton Mifflin, 1998. Poignant reflections on the psychology of rowing from a former collegiate and current masters rower.

Lehmann, R. C. *The Complete Oarsman.* London: Methuen, 1908. A history and manual of rowing and sculling. Although the recommended style (the so-called English Orthodox) is now long out of date, the book is fascinating as a period piece and for its splendid old photos.

Lewis, Brad. *Assult on Lake Casitas.* Philadelphia: Broad Street Books, 1990. Angry and passionate story of the author's successful quest for an Olympic medal.

Look, Margaret. *Courtney: Master Oarsman, Champion Coach.* Interlaken, NY: Empire State Books, 1989. A journalist who had

174 • *Suggested Readings*

access to unpublished archival material offers a succinct, readable account of Courtney's career.

Mendenhall, Thomas C. III. *A Short History of American Rowing.* Boston: Charles River Books, 1980. A literate, lively, and concise account by a rower, historian, and college president. The author notes that rowing is "a veritable religious experience for its devotees."

Morrison, J. S. and J. F. Coates, *The Athenian Trireme. The History and Reconstruction of an Ancient Greek Warship.* Cambridge: Cambridge University Press, 1986. An introduction to the history and reconstruction of the oared ship that, 2,500 years ago, was the backbone of the world's greatest navy. Scholarly but accessible to the general reader.

Paduda, Joe. *The Art of Sculling.* Camden, ME: Ragged Mountain Press, 1992. Excellent, practical introduction to all aspects of sculling, written with enthusiasm and sympathy. Particularly good on training drills.

Rankov, Boris. "Reconstructing the Past: The Operation of the Trireme Reconstruction, *Olympias,* In the Light of the Historical Sources." *Mariner's Mirror* (1994). The best discussion of what it might have felt like to have been an oarsman on an Athenian trireme around 400 B.C. The author, a professor of classics and a participant in the trireme reconstruction project, is himself a British rowing champion.

Shigematsu, Soiko, compiler and translator. *A Zen Forest. Sayings of the Masters.* New York: Weatherhill, 1981. Translations of short, memorable sayings that offer an introduction to an austere discipline. Includes an introductory essay and calligraphic illustrations.

Smith, Ronald A. *Sports and Freedom: The Rise of Big-time College Athletics.* New York: Oxford University Press, 1988. This readable history of sports both in and outside universities in late nineteenth- and early-twentieth-century America includes several chapters on rowing.

Strauss, Barry S. "The Athenian Trireme, School of Democracy." In J. Ober and C. Hedrick, eds. *Demokratia. A Conversa-*

tion on Democracies, Ancient and Modern. Princeton: Princeton University Press, 1996: 313–325. A scholarly discussion of the politics and sociology of the Athenian navy.

———— and Josiah Ober. *The Anatomy of Error. Ancient Military Disasters and Their Lessons for Modern Strategists.* New York: St. Martin's, 1990. Eight case studies of Greco-Roman warfare, among them various examples of naval warfare. Chapter two offers a concise history of the Peloponnesian War.

Tracy, Stephen. "The Panathenaic Festival: An Epigraphic Inquiry." *Nikephoros* 4 (1991): 133–153. This excellent analysis of the Parthenon sculpture discusses the importance of horses and horse-racing in classical Athenian life.

Woolf, Geoffrey. *The Final Club.* New York: Knopf, 1990. A coming-of-age novel about a diffident Princeton undergraduate in 1960 who finds himself through rowing.

Young, Charles Van Patten. *Courtney and Cornell Rowing.* Ithaca, NY, Cornell Publications Printing, 1923. A Cornell professor offers a detailed if sentimental account of his former colleague's life, including many quotations from Courtney. A period piece but engrossing.